Top Management Teams

Top Management Teams

How to Be Effective Inside and Outside the Boardroom

Anneloes M. L. Raes

University of St. Gallen

business**expert**
Press

First published in 2011 by
Business Expert Press, LLC
222 East 46th Street, New York, NY 10017
www.businessexpertpress.com

ISBN-13: 978-160649-179-9 (paperback)

ISBN-13: 978-160649-180-5 (e-book)

Parts of chapter 3 are adapted from "The Interface of the Top Manage-
ment Team and Middle Managers: A Process Model," by Raes, A. M.
L., Heijltjes, M. G., Glunk, U., & Roe, R. A., 2011, *Academy of Manage-
ment Review, 36*(1), pp. 102–126, and are reprinted with permission.
Parts of chapter 4 are adapted from "Top Management Team and Middle
Managers: Making Sense of Leadership," by Raes, A. M. L., Glunk, U.,
Heijltjes, M. G., & Roe, R. A., 2007, *Small Group Research, 38*(3), pp.
360–386, and are reprinted with permission.

DOI 10.4128/9781606491805

A publication in the Business Expert Press Strategic Management
collection

Collection ISSN: 2150-9611 (print)
Collection ISSN: 2150-9646 (electronic)

Cover design by Jonathan Pennell
Interior design by Scribe Inc.

First edition: September 2011

10 9 8 7 6 5 4 3 2 1

Printed in the United States of America.

Abstract

A top management team (TMT) matters for its organization, right? While researchers have established that TMTs do "matter," the ways in which TMTs do that are complex and opaque. This book outlines how a TMT can matter most for its organization, and it does so in a positive way by considering the most recent academic and practical insights. Two factors are critical: (1) inside the boardroom, TMT members' behavior determines the quality of strategic decisions, and (2) outside the board-room, the way in which the TMT works with middle managers is crucial for the subsequent implementation of those decisions. Understanding how these two factors can be effectively performed can help TMT members, middle managers, team coaches, HR practitioners, and so on to grasp the complex mechanisms of TMT impact.

Keywords

Top management team, middle managers, organizational performance, organizational impact, strategic decision making

Contents

Preface

How can top management teams (TMTs) be more effective? With this deceivingly simple question, I started doing research on TMTs about 7 years ago. I was particularly interested in the way in which the TMT members interact while doing their work, as some important scientific studies on this topic had just appeared. But what I had envisioned as a main explanation for TMT effectiveness quickly turned out to be that notorious tip of the iceberg.

This blind spot in the TMT literature occurred to me for the first time when I was observing the weekly board meetings of a particular TMT. This TMT seemingly did everything right with regard to its interaction processes: The TMT members had many intense, task-related discussions but few interpersonal fights. They openly shared information and opinions but had few political games and behind-the-scenes coalitions. They even had special sessions every month to reflect on their functioning and processes. These were in addition to the yearly 3-day strategy-building sessions, of course.

This TMT was everything a team coach would advise a TMT to be. But still it was questioning how to become more effective. TMT members were struggling with how to have a real impact on the organization. And they were puzzled with why their strategic decisions would sometimes not achieve the effects that they had envisioned. Despite the usual organizational reporting mechanisms, the existence of monetary and nonmonetary incentives, and even the TMT members' internal unity, the TMT had a difficult time getting their strategic decisions to "work."

Based on the difficulties that this TMT experienced during the observation period, I started to develop a new research focus: the relationship between the TMT and middle managers. I firmly believe that this relationship is key in allowing strategic decisions to take effect. When a TMT uses interactions with middle managers well, it can gain valuable new perspectives and information and create real commitment to getting decisions implemented. If things do not work well, middle managers have many different options to delay strategy implementation or even to sabotage it.

This book provides insight into how TMTs can be effective both in their internal processes and in the way in which they work with middle managers. It builds upon the most recent academic and practical insights. The book is intended for TMT members, nonexecutive directors, consultants, or team coaches, as well as general readers who are curious to learn more about the mechanisms TMTs use to influence their organizations.

Several findings from our projects have been published in various academic journals. With this book, I hope to make this knowledge more accessible to those working in practice. To help readers begin applying the knowledge, each chapter starts with a short introduction and ends with concrete questions that can help readers distill the key insights of the chapters.

This book reports findings from a series of research projects. All projects were performed in close cooperation with Robert Roe, Mariëlle Heijltjes, and Urusla Glunk from Maastricht University in the Netherlands. Even though they insisted on my name being the only one on the book's cover, this book simply would not have existed without their input and encouragement. Thank you!

Anneloes Raes, April 2011

CHAPTER 1

Teams at the Top

A top management team (TMT) matters for its organization, right? This assumption is widespread among both researchers and practitioners. In fact, it underlies many far-reaching decisions, such as rewarding team members for great organizational performance or firing them for poor performance. While researchers have established that TMTs do "matter" for their organizations,[1] the ways in which TMTs do that are complex and opaque.

The mechanisms of TMT impact evolve along a complex interplay of both strategic and psychological processes. This complexity can make it difficult for TMTs, and those around them, to see what it really takes to make them "work" for their organizations. In this book, I outline two sources of TMT impact: what happens inside the boardroom, when TMT members are among themselves, and what happens outside, when TMT members interact with others.

Inside the boardroom, I describe the social and psychological processes that shape the way in which TMTs make decisions. Outside the boardroom, I address how TMTs can effectively work with middle managers and achieve high-quality strategic decisions along with effective implementation. To get more insight into the particular challenges that TMTs face, I will first describe some typical characteristics of TMTs and their work.

What Is a TMT?

Many people still credit organizational performance to the decisions of a heroic, single CEO. CEOs, so it is assumed, steer organizations according to a "one-captain-on-a-ship" approach. They are the ones to be credited for successes or blamed for losses. Yet organizational reality is that many organizations nowadays have a TMT instead of a single decision maker at the top.[2] That is, the CEO creates a team of executives around him or her, and strategic decisions are made within the team.

The concept of TMT was introduced in the organizational literature more than 20 years ago by Hambrick and Mason.[3] These authors simply referred to a TMT as "the firm's officers." More recently, researchers have specified a TMT to be "the aggregate informational and decisional entity through which the organization operates and which forms the inner circle of executives who collectively formulate, articulate, and execute the strategic and tactical moves of the organization."[4]

As these definitions imply, the TMT is the group of executive managers highest in the organizational hierarchy. Such an organizational position implies, among many other things, that these managers have much freedom in the way they plan and execute their work. They also have to deal with a constant stream of unstructured information. Often they are faced with high time pressure for making decisions.[5]

Why would your organization want a team at the top? Does it actually need a team? And is it even realistic to expect such a thing as a team at the highest organizational echelon? Some researchers and managers argue that TMTs have little "teamness" to them and are in fact only a collection of strong players or a group of "semi-autonomous barons."[6] On the other hand, recent research has indicated that many organizations do have "real teams" at the top.[7]

A TMT can be seen as a real team when it is a distinct organizational entity, has clearly defined members, is reasonably stable in membership over time, and has members who are interdependent in their work.[8] The prevalence of TMTs that work as real teams also seems to expand in response to the turbulence and complexity of the current global business environment of many organizations.[9]

In line with these developments, I focus in this book on TMTs that have at least a minimal level of teamness. That is, the TMT is seen by TMT members and others as a distinct organizational entity, has clearly defined members, is reasonably stable in membership over time, and has members who carry out its work with some level of interdependence.[10] The extent to which these TMTs also show behavioral processes that indicate high levels of teamness will be further discussed in chapter 2, along with the performance consequences.

The TMT's Strategic Work

A main objective of the TMT's work is to formulate and implement strategic decisions that ensure the survival and growth of the organization.[11] Strategic decision making consists of the choice of a particular course of strategic action. Strategy implementation comprises the subsequent actions to make that strategy happen.[12] The TMT's work of formulating and implementing strategy implies that the tasks of a TMT are more complex and varied than those of most other teams. TMT members must comprehend a great deal of vague, ambiguous, and often conflicting information.[13]

To formulate and implement high-quality decisions, the TMT is dependent on many other people both inside and outside the organization. The TMT's interactions with others are therefore a particularly important aspect of its work. This exposure to many other people also implies that a TMT is highly visible for others both inside and outside the organization. Hence its actions carry symbolic meaning and tend to be closely watched, and discussed, by other managers and employees.[14]

Finally, TMTs often consist of members from different parts of the organization, such that these members are simultaneously part of the TMT and the heads of their own business units.[15] Therefore, TMT members' priorities, languages, and values are usually quite different from each other.[16] These specific characteristics of the TMT create promises but also some pitfalls.

Promises and Pitfalls

Working as a team instead of individually is often preferred when work is too voluminous or too complex to be performed alone. Teams have the advantage of being flexible in how they deploy and use their resources, and they provide opportunities for team members to learn from one another.[17] This is clearly the case for work at the top of organizations. Researchers have stated that the current organizational reality is often too complex for a single manager to oversee. A division of tasks among TMT members in a team structure can provide a way for dealing with this complexity.[18]

Researchers have proposed that by working in a TMT, the quality of strategic decisions can be increased because multiple managers can apply more diverse perspectives to solve a problem.[19] The synthesis of these perspectives is expected to be superior to an individual's decision.[20] The executives' commitment to implement decisions can increase through the understanding and acceptance generated by joint decision-making processes.[21] In addition, having a TMT at the top instead of a single manager has the potential to improve communication and cooperation among executives from different subunits.

Despite the theoretical advantages of having a team at the top, effective TMT functioning is not self-evident. According to psychological theories, the same diversity in perspectives and information that can produce better decisions may also impair the interpersonal relationships of TMT members.[22] These theories would therefore suggest that *similarity* in perspectives would in fact be desirable for maintaining a positive atmosphere in the TMT.

Yet, on the other hand, too much similarity in perspectives may lead to the phenomenon called groupthink, when senior teams strive for high consensus at the expense of good decisions.[23] Thus, in addition to the uncertainty and complexity associated with strategic decision making, doing that in a team setting presents extra challenges and the potential for problems that relate to interpersonal issues.

Because TMT functioning itself is challenging, it may also be easy to forget that an important aspect of TMT work is to manage relationships with others. Such relationships with other stakeholders both inside and outside the organization serve as channels of information and influence. Researchers have shown that the quantity, quality, and diversity of TMT members' relationships to others can be linked to organizational performance.[24] Therefore, an additional pitfall is that the TMT does not pay enough attention to systematically managing the relationships to others.

TMT Impact on the Organization

How can a TMT reap the benefits and avoid the traps of working in a team? Assuming that "good" performance of a TMT translates into an organization performing well, researchers have investigated which characteristics of the TMT matter the most for organizational performance. Two streams of research provide primary insight into these questions:

research from the upper-echelons perspective in the strategy discipline and team research from the social and organizational psychology fields.

Composition of the Team

Scholars of strategy have studied TMTs from the perspective of the upper-echelons theory.[25] This theory emphasizes the role of TMT composition in terms of TMT members' demographic characteristics, such as age or functional background, for explaining organizational performance. TMTs with demographically diverse members are proposed to have more capabilities for processing information than TMTs whose members are similar, and this diversity is expected to benefit strategic decision making and organizational performance.[26]

Despite much empirical work, the results of studies that link TMT composition to organizational performance have been quite inconsistent until recently.[27] As a result, researchers have repeatedly concluded that considering TMT composition alone does not provide real insight into how TMTs influence organizational performance.[28] Some have even suggested to "call a moratorium for the use of demographic variables as surrogates for psychological constructs."[29]

For those readers interested in reading more on the role of TMT composition, some excellent reviews exist.[30] In the remainder of this book, I focus on the role of the TMT's internal processes and states, as well as the TMT's relationships to middle managers.

Internal Processes and States

Researchers have proposed that TMT performance is affected not so much by the composition of the TMT as by the way in which TMT members use and combine their differences. Because TMT effectiveness may vary from situation to situation but TMT composition changes only infrequently, they reasoned that other processes must also be at work to explain effectiveness. To better understand these processes, researchers have built on theories about nonmanagerial teams from social and organizational psychology. In these fields, the interactions between members of small groups have long been of central interest.[31]

Team internal processes describe the nature of the TMT members' interaction and behavior while working on achieving the team's goals,[32] whereas team emergent states are the cognitive and affective modes of a team at a certain moment.[33] TMT researchers have studied both internal processes and emergent states to understand how team inputs are transferred to outcomes and potential mediators and moderators of TMT composition-organizational performance relationships.[34]

In this book, I focus on the role of TMT processes and states in what happens inside the boardroom, where the TMT makes strategic decisions, and in what happens outside, where the TMT works with others to ensure the subsequent implementation of these decisions.

Relationship to Middle Managers

Middle managers are those managers who work in the management layer between the TMT and first-level supervisors, such as managers of divisions or subsidiaries.[35] Because middle managers have both upward and downward influence, researchers have called them "linking pins" in the organization.[36] In this role, middle managers have the power to delay, speed up, block, or support strategy formulation and implementation.[37]

As linking pins, middle managers also make sense of what happens in the organization. Their interpretations of organization events are an important source of information for the TMT. On the other hand, when middle managers interpret what happens in the TMT and share their conclusions with their own employees, they can easily influence how employees in the organization as a whole think about the TMT.[38] Because middle managers have such an important function, top managers heavily depend on them to achieve organizational goals.[39] Therefore, it is an important aspect of TMT work to gain middle managers' commitment to, or at least compliance with, the TMT's courses of action.

In this book, I describe what can make the interaction between the TMT and middle managers successful. I also present the results of an in-depth case study on how a TMT understands its relationship to middle managers. Finally, I switch to the middle manager perspective and examine what middle managers expect from their TMT and how they evaluate it.

The Structure of This Book

Chapter 2: Inside the Boardroom—TMT Behavior

In this chapter, I focus on TMTs' internal behavioral processes. In particular, I present what researchers have discovered regarding the organization-wide consequences of specific TMT processes and states. I first distinguish between different aspects of TMT behavior: those aspects that are more task oriented and those that are more relationship oriented. Then I consider how these task- and relationship-oriented aspects of TMT behavior can influence the quality of the TMT's strategic decisions, the TMT's performance, and the performance of the organization as a whole.

Chapter 3: Outside the Boardroom—The Relationship Between the TMT and Middle Managers

In chapter 3, I outline how TMTs can achieve maximum benefits from their interactions with middle managers. I outline a recently developed model on this topic called the "interface model." This model explains which aspects of the interactions between the TMT and middle managers are particularly crucial for strategy formulation and implementation. I then describe how the usually scarce moments of contact between the two groups can be used to align their actions. The model then outlines what TMTs and middle managers can do to achieve a successful "interface."

Chapter 4: TMT Sensemaking About Middle Managers

To effectively deal with middle managers, TMT members need to agree on their approach toward them. In chapter 4, I present the results of an in-depth case study that addresses this topic. To understand how this TMT worked on achieving a unified view of its approach toward middle managers, I use the concept of "sensemaking" to analyze the TMT members' interactions.

Chapter 5: Middle Manager Perspectives

To make the interaction between the TMT and middle managers work, it is also helpful to understand the other side of the coin—that is, middle managers' perspective on their TMT. Therefore, in this chapter I present the results of an empirical study in which the expectations and evaluations of middle managers were assessed on five dimensions: company results, strategic leadership, connectedness, TMT unity, and moral leadership. Interestingly, there were some clear discrepancies between what middle managers expected from their TMT and how they evaluated it.

Chapter 6: Making It Work

In this chapter, I integrate the insights presented in the previous chapters. This way, TMTs and those working with them get some clear recommendations for their behavior both inside and outside the boardroom.

Make It Work for Your TMT

1. What is the level of teamness of your TMT?
2. What are the particular promises and pitfalls of your TMT?
3. Which (groups of) people are particularly key to your TMT's impact?
4. How would you describe the relationship between TMT and middle managers in your organization?

CHAPTER 2

Inside the Boardroom

TMT Behavior

The behavior of top management team (TMT) members inside the boardroom has organization-wide consequences. But which aspects of this behavior are most important? In this chapter, I describe what researchers have discovered to answer this question.

Inside the boardroom, TMT members work together to make strategic and operational decisions. They also decide how to implement those decisions and discuss a wide variety of monitoring and control issues.[1] While working on these tasks, their interaction varies over time: At one moment there may be intense discussions between TMT members with many opposing viewpoints and interests, while at another they may agree on a certain course of action without much further discussion.

TMTs may also differ in how their members interact. In one TMT, members may get along well with much agreement and a positive atmosphere, whereas another TMT is characterized by constant conflict and aggression. Although TMT behavior varies over time, depending, for example, on situation-specific distributions of information and interests,[2] it is possible get an overview of the general characteristics of this behavior.

In this chapter, I first explain how TMT behavior can be analyzed along task and relationship dimensions and the differences between processes and states. I then outline the three ways that researchers have used to analyze TMT performance. And based on the most recent academic insights, I then analyze which processes and states have a profound impact on TMT performance.

TMT Behavior: Processes and States

When analyzing TMT behavior inside the boardroom, there are many aspects that one could potentially focus on. But how do you know which aspects are central? To get an overview of these different aspects and their effects, researchers have made a distinction between so-called task processes, relationship processes, and emergent states.[3] This distinction allows both researchers and practitioners to be precise about what it is that they are interested in. Moreover, the distinction helps to pinpoint exactly how various aspects of TMT behavior relate to organizational outcomes.

Task processes describe characteristics of TMT members' interaction and behavior that relate to the work task of the TMT. For example, researchers have studied processes of "task conflict" and "dissent" to refer to the extent to which TMT interaction is characterized by task-related discussions and differences in opinions. When task conflict is high, TMT members have frequent and intense discussions about the content of work and about what decisions to make. In contrast, when task conflict is low, TMT members generally agree with each other and come to a consensus quickly.

Relationship processes describe how TMT members relate to each other. An example of such a process is "relationship conflict," which describes the extent to which there are interpersonal tensions and animosities between the TMT members. If there is a high level of relationship conflict, TMT members have frequent fights with each other that are accompanied by discussions that focus on the person rather than the content of work. If relationship conflict is low, there are few of these personal fights.

Team emergent states describe the state that a TMT is in at a certain moment. An emergent state does not directly capture an aspect of behavior but rather captures an underlying "mood" of a TMT. It may entail both affective and cognitive aspects. That is, emergent states can describe both how TMT members *feel* about the TMT and how they *think* about it. An example of such an emergent state is cohesion. If a TMT is high in cohesion, TMT members feel attracted to the TMT and typically stick together. When TMT cohesion is low, TMT members do not feel particularly attached to the team and do their own jobs with little consideration of the other TMT members.

Task processes, relationship processes, and emergent states may occur in different combinations in different TMTs. One TMT may have extremely intense task-related discussions with few interpersonal fights because all TMT members feel attached to the team and are fully committed to make the best possible decisions. In contrast, another TMT may also have intense discussions about the task, but here the initially purely work-related discussions spill over into high levels of interpersonal conflicts.

Many different types of processes and emergent states have been studied in the past 20 years. And they have been related to different types of organizational outcomes. That is, researchers have attempted to analyze which processes and states are more or less desirable by relating them to various indicators of how well an organization is doing. These typical outcomes are now addressed first before examining their exact relationships with processes and states.

Three Indicators for TMT Performance

The TMT Makes "Good" Decisions

The first category of outcomes refers to the decisions that the TMT makes. Since making and implementing strategic decisions are key aspects of TMT work, researchers have found it of particular interest to assess the extent to which TMT decisions fulfill important criteria. For example, researchers have focused on the concept of "decision quality." It is arguably difficult to provide an exact assessment of the quality of a strategic decision. Researchers have nevertheless suggested that the quality of a strategic decision can be analyzed by considering the extent to which the content of a decision is in line with environmental demands and the organization's mission, is financially responsible, and is timely.[4] Other examples of criteria relating to the strategic decisions of the TMT include TMT members' acceptance of the decision and their commitment to implementing it.

The TMT Performs Well as a Group

The second category of outcomes relates to how the TMT functions as a group. When the TMT performs well as a group, it is effective in combining the input of the TMT members and achieving the TMT's goals. In these TMTs, you will also typically see that the group processes meet TMT members' needs for growth and satisfaction and that the TMT enhances their capability to work together in the future.[5]

The Organization Performs Well

Probably the most obvious criterion for how a TMT performs is the success of the organization as a whole, and this is what most researchers have assessed. The performance of organizations can be measured by a variety of indicators. Many researchers have focused on common financial indicators, such as return on assets, profit, and return on investments. Some others have focused on more intangible aspects, such as innovation or corporate venturing. Still others have taken a slightly different approach and have measured indicators of *bad* performance, such as organizational decline.[6]

TMT Processes: Making Tasks and Relationships Work

How Can Task Processes Influence Performance?

Researchers who are interested in task-related aspects of TMT behavior have focused on the so-called task processes—those characteristics of TMT members' interaction and behavior that directly relate to the contents of work. Task processes are of clear interest for understanding TMT performance because they describe "what" the TMT members do.

To understand how these task processes can influence performance, many researchers have used the theory of information processing. This theory focuses on how information flows between different TMT members and which TMT behaviors help or hinder the information exchange.[7] Since information exchange is a key aspect of what TMT members do, this theory applies particularly well to understanding how effective they are.

The underlying rationale of information-processing theory rests on the notion of "bounded rationality."[8] This concept describes how all top managers—and, indeed, all people—are subject to particular perceptual filters and biases that shape what they notice in their environment. Such biases can hardly be prevented, as the sheer volume of the information that top managers need to process makes it impossible to give every piece of information the same amount of attention and consideration.

Although all members of a TMT are subject to this bounded rationality, their particular filters and biases are likely to be different. This is likely because people's biases and filters are shaped by their values and experiences—ranging from TMT members' current organizational position to their study background or even non-work-related experiences, such as growing up in a particular time period or environment.

TMT members' wide range of biases in perception and judgment is a clear advantage to the quality of the TMT's decisions, according to the advocates of information processing theory. When TMT members use decision processes in which they exchange their perspectives, the effects of a single top manager's biases and filters will be reduced. TMT interaction processes that are characterized by extensive information exchange should thus enhance the quality of the TMT's decisions. Hence researchers have proclaimed that TMT task processes characterized by differentiation in information and opinions will lead to the incorporation of more and more diverse information, the generation of creative ideas and multiple alternatives, and the application of the diverse skills and experience that TMT members possess.[9]

Based on the theory of information processing, researchers have studied a wide variety of task processes. The aim was always to analyze how specific types of task processes would predict one or more of the three aspects of TMT performance—the TMT makes good decisions, the TMT performs well as a group, and the organization performs well. I will now describe the results of three types of task processes: task conflict, behavioral integration, and communication frequency.

Task Conflict: To Disagree or Not to Disagree?

The process of "task conflict" has been studied most often, sometimes under a slightly different name, such as dissent or debate.[10] Task conflict is the extent to which there are disagreements among TMT members about the content of the task being performed, including differences in viewpoints, ideas, and opinions. In general, researchers have concluded that task conflict is a particularly beneficial process for TMTs.

TMTs with high levels of task conflict make higher-quality decisions than TMTs with lower levels of such task conflict.[11] TMT members' understanding and acceptance of these decisions also increases, as does their commitment to subsequently implement the decisions.[12] Finally, the comprehensiveness of the decision process also increases with high levels of task conflict.[13] Interestingly, the speed of decision making seems not to be compromised when TMT members engage in extensive task-related discussions.[14]

Task conflict is beneficial not only for the quality of the TMT's decisions but also for the way in which a TMT performs as a group.[15] When a large amount of task-related disagreements exist in a TMT, these TMT members do a better job than those in a team with little disagreement, with respect to leveraging the benefits of working in a team structure. Thus, for making good decisions and functioning well as a team, it seems advisable for a TMT to exhibit a decision process with extensive discussion and disagreement. But do these beneficial effects also translate into better performance of the organization as a whole?

Unfortunately, when considering the effect of TMT task conflict on the way in which the organization performs, the picture is more complicated. Some researchers have shown that task conflict is related to higher organizational profit and growth.[16] However, these effects were mostly found in a context of young, entrepreneurial organizations rather than in more established organizations. In many other studies, researchers found no relationship between the TMT's task conflict and organizational performance.[17]

These results may be puzzling at first sight. When the TMT's decisions are good and the TMT members perform well as a group, why would this not translate into a high-performing organization? There may be many answers to this question, but I believe that an important aspect to consider is decision implementation. Even when a TMT generates high-quality decisions by having many task-related disagreements, if it does not subsequently implement this decision, it is unlikely that the organization as a whole will benefit.

Research has shown that about half of the strategic decisions in organizations fail to achieve the intended effects. Moreover, the main causes of these failures occur during decision implementation rather than decision making.[18] And these causes are generally under management control instead of resulting from uncontrollable external factors.[19] In the next chapters, I will therefore focus on the alignment between the TMT and its middle managers as an important way to achieve decision implementation. But first, I consider other task-related aspects of the TMT's internal processes.

Behavioral Integration: Working as a Team

Researchers have also studied other task-related aspects of the TMT's interaction. One of the most interesting processes at the moment is called "behavioral integration." This construct describes the extent to which a TMT makes joint decisions, openly shares information and opinions, and carries out the work collectively.[20] It is interesting because it says something about how a TMT has chosen to approach its work.

People often have reservations about the extent to which a TMT can really function as a team, what I called in chapter 1 the issue of the "teamness" of TMTs. The notion that leadership is an individual act is deeply embedded in people's understanding. It is fueled by images of the great leaders of our time, which dutifully portray these men and women as the great individuals they are or were. But the fact that these leaders worked with great teams of people around them—sharing decisions, taking advice, and creating synergies—is hardly ever mentioned.[21]

With the focus on TMT behavioral integration, researchers have clearly shown that it pays off for a TMT to work as an integrated collective. Behavioral integration has important positive relations not only to decision quality[22] but also to multiple indicators of organizational performance.[23] The work on TMT knowledge sharing supports this line of research, as the extent to which a TMT shares knowledge is related to the organization's performance.

This indicates that it is a good thing for a TMT when decisions are made jointly rather than by the CEO only. It shows that openly sharing information and opinions within the TMT should be promoted rather than having TMT members engage in political processes to enhance influence on decisions. And it demonstrates that carrying out the work collectively—indeed, as a "real team"—is also beneficial at the top.

It should be noted that some research has failed to show that TMT behavioral integration is beneficial, as researchers could not relate it to enhanced service quality[24] and corporate entrepreneurship.[25] But all in all, having a TMT that is high in behavioral integration is at least never a bad thing. The research on behavioral integration is a promising new line of research and suggests that working as a team at the top actually "works."

Communication: The More the Better?

If a TMT should have many task-related discussions and should function as a behaviorally integrated team, does this imply that TMT members should spend as much time as possible communicating with each other? How can they achieve that when they have a multitude of responsibilities beyond those of the TMT, with only a limited amount of time and energy? Luckily, the literature suggests that it is not so much about the frequency of communication as it is about the quality.

Studies that have investigated processes of TMT communication indicate that more frequent communication, as compared with less frequent communication, is not related to better outcomes.[26] In fact, one study suggests that more frequent communication is related to lower organizational growth and return on investment.[27] Another study found no relationship between the frequency of the TMT's information exchange and firm performance.[28] Thus it seems that it is not so much the frequency of communication that counts but rather the quality of communication at the relatively scarce moments of contact between TMT members.

Relationship Processes: Relationship Conflict

The research presented so far clearly suggests that differences in information and opinions between TMT members provide an advantage for a TMT. Unfortunately, they may also provide disadvantages. The theory of information exchange provides a positive perspective on the effects of discussions, debate, and task conflict for the TMT's decisions and performance, but the theories of social identity and similarity attraction paint a different picture.

Based on psychological insights into how people construct and maintain their identity in social settings, these theories predict that interpersonal relationships are more satisfying and effective if they are characterized by similarities between different people. This effect occurs because such similarities confirm the value and appropriateness of one's own opinions and perspectives, through which people gain a positive view of themselves.

These psychological tendencies are also at work in TMTs. Even though "being a TMT member" is only one aspect of an executive's identity (in addition to, for example, being a parent, a church member, a mountain climber, and a jazz musician), these psychological tendencies are pervasive in all aspects of life, including TMT work. In addition, it is in fact a crucial aspect of TMT success to achieve consensus on a new strategy, to formulate decisions that all members can work with, and to maintain a sense of unity toward others—all aspects that benefit from similarity in opinions and perspectives. Therefore, *differences* in opinion and perspectives are quite likely to spill over to relationship-oriented, detrimental conflict.

Relationship conflict is problematic for TMT performance because it wastes and misapplies TMT members' time and energy. With the notion of "process losses," Steiner[29] has described the coordination and motivation difficulties that cause a team to perform worse than could be expected based on the individual team members' knowledge and skills. When the relationship processes between TMT members create such process losses, negative effects on TMT performance can be expected.[30]

These theoretical expectations are confirmed by existing empirical work. Relationship conflict has been related to lower decision quality and affective acceptance of these decisions.[31] It has also been related to lower organizational performance.[32] In some instances, relationship conflict did not exert such negative effects on decisions and performance outcomes,[33] but it was clearly not beneficial as well.

TMT Processes: How to Make Them Work

The research on TMT processes provides some clear suggestions for TMTs. First, disagreements on tasks between TMT members are beneficial to the quality of the TMT's decisions, as well as to TMT members' understanding of and commitment to these decisions. But since it is unlikely that such task conflict directly translates into better organizational performance, TMTs need to ensure subsequent implementation of those decisions. How to do this is the topic of chapter 3.

Second, TMTs that make joint decisions, openly share information and opinions, and collectively carry out their work outperform TMTs that do not function as such an integrated collective, in terms of both decisions and organizational performance. Apparently, there is something to a behaviorally integrated TMT that also facilitates decision implementation, which task conflict does not have.

Third, TMTs do not need to interact very frequently to achieve the benefits of task conflict and behavioral integration. In fact, frequent TMT communication may take away much-needed time and energy from other activities. Achieving a high quality of information exchange, but not at the expense of frequent meetings, seems to be a key characteristic of successful TMTs.

Fourth, relationship conflict is not beneficial for decision quality and organizational performance. Even though it does not always do harm, it never helps and therefore should be avoided when possible.

So, in sum, the recommendation must be that TMTs share information and opinions and stimulate task-related disagreements but avoid relationship-oriented conflicts, right? This is clearly the right answer based on the scientific research presented so far. Unfortunately, combining these two beneficial processes is in practice not so easy. Because task and relationship aspects of TMT interaction are usually interrelated, beneficial task conflicts can easily spill over to disruptive relationship conflict.[34]

The question of how this spillover effect can be avoided has been the focus of some recent studies on the "states" of TMTs. I will therefore first describe some characteristics of these TMT emergent states and then address how emergent states, such as trust and norms, can help TMTs achieve effective interaction processes.

TMT Emergent States

The concept of the "emergent state" is relatively new to the TMT literature.[35] It describes the underlying "mood" of a TMT. The state in which a TMT is at a certain moment—for example, one of high trust—influences the way in which the TMT members discuss a new strategy. And based on what happens during this discussion, TMT members may adapt their level of trust. Although the concept of the emergent state is new, researchers have already addressed multiple different states, among which are social cohesion and trust.

Social Cohesion

Social cohesion describes the TMT members' attraction to the team that reflects their shared commitment and team pride.[36] Researchers have also called this state "social integration" or simply "cohesion."[37] Although too much cohesion may also pose a danger to groups,[38] in the current TMT literature, researchers have found mostly positive effects.

Social cohesion is related to enhanced TMT effectiveness,[39] TMT action aggressiveness,[40] and organizations' growth in sales and return on investment.[41] Thus TMTs whose members are attracted to the team, are committed to its purposes, and feel proud to be part of it have clear advantages over TMTs that are in a state of low cohesion.

Trust

Trust is a TMT member's willingness to be vulnerable toward another TMT member in the absence of a direct possibility to monitor the other.[42] Even though one would generally assume that the TMT members' trust in each other is a good thing, the research findings are slightly more complicated. Trust is good not because it directly leads to beneficial outcomes,[43] but because it allows a TMT to have beneficial task conflict while avoiding detrimental relationship conflict.[44]

A study by Simons and Peterson[45] nicely illustrates the underlying mechanism for this function. When a TMT is in a state of high trust, task conflicts stay what they are: content-related discussions about the decision at hand. But when there is low trust, TMT members interpret a difference in opinion as a potential personal attack and react accordingly, with a counterargument that relates more to the person than to the issue at hand. This way, what started as a legitimate—and in fact very beneficial—task conflict spills over into a detrimental relationship conflict. Having a high level of trust among TMT members prevents this from happening.

Inside the Boardroom: Concluding Remarks

It is not easy for researchers to get TMTs to talk about, and systematically analyze, what happens inside the boardroom. But they have managed to do so, perhaps because executives also see the value of systematic, scientific knowledge about how TMT behavior relates to important outcomes. And researchers have obtained good results; several studies have illustrated that the TMT's internal processes and states matter for outcomes.

Most notably, task conflict and behavioral integration are clearly to be stimulated, but excessive communication and relationship conflict are to be avoided. The emergent states of trust and team norms can facilitate these beneficial processes. For TMTs in practice, the challenge is to closely reflect on what happens in their own boardrooms and use these scientific insights to analyze and optimize their own dynamics.

Make It Work for Your TMT

1. Which task processes are most apparent in the interactions of your TMT?
2. Which relationship processes are present in your TMT?
3. Could you analyze the dominant "mood," or emergent state, of your TMT?
4. Do you see a relationship between the interaction processes in your TMT and the quality of strategic decisions?

5. Do you see a relationship between the interaction processes in your TMT and the way in which the TMT functions as a group?

6. Does your TMT exhibit the beneficial processes of task conflict and behavioral integration and avoid the dysfunctional processes of excessive communication and relationship conflict?

7. What are the levels of social cohesion and trust in your TMT?

CHAPTER 3

Outside the Boardroom

The Relationship Between the TMT and Middle Managers

It is the pattern of relationships within organizations, not the fact that "great men" sit at the top of them, which makes it possible to exert influence and enhance organizational performance.

—K. E. Weick, *The Social Psychology of Organizing*

Top management teams (TMTs) do not work in a social vacuum. In fact, as Karl Weick's quote illustrates, top managers impact the organization largely through their relationships with others. Inside the organization, the TMT interacts, for example, with middle managers, employees, and the board of directors. Outside the organization, the TMT may interact with clients, politicians, competitors, alliance partners, government agencies, and others.

Although it is evident that relationships with others are key for TMTs, TMT researchers have paid surprisingly little attention to this aspect of TMT work. For individual top managers, there is research available focusing on their networks, but little is known about the relationships that the TMT exercises with others. This observation was the start of a research program at Maastricht University in the Netherlands, in which researchers have focused on the relationship between the TMT and middle managers. The full report of this study has been published in the *Academy of Management Review* in 2011.[1]

In this chapter, I report the key findings of this study. My aim is to provide insight into some of the key characteristics of a successful alignment of the TMT and middle managers, or what the researchers have called the "interface of TMT and middle managers." But first, I will focus on why middle managers are so important for the TMT.

Why Are Middle Managers So Important for the TMT?

TMTs exert influence on organizational performance through the strategic decisions they make and implement. For both strategy making and implementation, top managers rely on their relationships with others, who serve as channels of information and influence.[2] A particularly crucial group is middle managers, those managers that function in the organizational layer between the TMT and first-level supervisors.[3]

Middle managers are organizational "linking pins" because their actions have both upward and downward influence in organizations.[4] As such, middle managers have the power to delay strategy implementation, reduce the quality of implementation, or even sabotage it.[5] They can also influence how other people in the organization think about the TMT via their "sensemaking" function vis-à-vis subordinates—that is, the way in which these subordinates interpret and understand the information they get about the TMT.[6] Through this function, they influence the trust that their subordinates have in the TMT.[7] Therefore, top managers depend on middle managers for achieving organizational goals and thus need to gain middle managers' commitment to their course of action.

Scholars studying middle managers have emphasized their roles in both strategy making and implementation.[8] Middle managers can influence strategy making by synthesizing information, championing alternatives,[9] and selling issues to top management.[10] Middle managers can influence strategy implementation because they put the strategy into practice and facilitate it as necessary. The involvement of middle managers in strategy has also been associated with increased organizational performance.[11] On the negative side, when middle managers are not committed to implementation, they can create obstacles or sabotage it.[12]

In our research, we have used the notion of "interface" to describe the situation where TMT and middle managers operate in the relatively separate worlds of their own tasks and responsibilities—worlds that intersect at specific moments. The interface can therefore be seen as an alternation of episodes of contact between the TMT and middle managers during which interactions, or "interface processes," take place, and periods of no contact, during which the TMT and middle managers act on their own on the basis of assumptions, expectations, and roles.

Asymmetry of Information, Interests, and Influence

The TMT and middle managers depend on each other for strategy formulation and implementation. But the parties are not equally powerful; there are asymmetries of information and influence. The TMT has the formal power base of its organizational function and an overview of a wide array of information from many intra- and extraorganizational sources.[13] The TMT has an additional power base because it can decide which middle managers it hires and promotes as well as with which middle managers it wants to interact for particular issues.[14]

Middle managers, on the other hand, usually have good access to intraorganizational information from lower echelons and are the first in line to work with the TMT's decisions.[15] They can also influence the TMT by selling issues, taking the initiative, and exercising their voices, by which they gain the TMT's attention.[16] Therefore, the power base of middle managers rests on their function as linking pins.

Given the different organizational functions of the TMT and middle managers, there is often an asymmetry in the *interests* of the two parties because middle managers pursue goals in the primary interest of their business units.[17] These are not necessarily fully in line with the goals of the TMT.

In the absence of complete information and with possibly divergent interests of the TMT and middle managers, each party experiences a certain amount of risk.[18] The TMT experiences risk in relying on the information from middle managers as a base for strategy formulation because this information may to some degree reflect middle managers' self-interest or the business unit's interest.[19] Middle managers experience risk in sharing their information and perspectives with the TMT, since they do not know whether the TMT will use the information they provide to their advantage or disadvantage.[20]

The TMT, as the most powerful party in the relationship, will reduce its risk by exercising formal control mechanisms to obtain middle managers' information and compliance.[21] But middle managers have a considerable degree of freedom in the extent to which they allow the TMT to influence them.[22] Nevertheless, because the strategy process is so complex and uncertain, full control by any one entity is not possible by definition.[23]

When risk and interdependency coexist in a relationship, trust becomes important as a driver of the behavior of the two parties toward each other.[24] Researchers have formally defined *trust* as

> the willingness of a party to be vulnerable to the actions of another party based on the expectation that the other will perform a particular action important to the trustor, irrespective of the ability to monitor or control that other party.[25]

Because it is impossible for the TMT and middle managers to constantly monitor each other's actions, their trust in each other is of key importance. Before describing which behaviors are particularly relevant for trust, I will now address which key processes characterize the interactions of the TMT and middle managers.

Key Processes Between the TMT and Middle Managers

Information Exchange

TMT researchers have often built on information-processing theory—introduced in chapter 2—to suggest that strategic decision quality is influenced by the amount and type of information that the TMT gathers, interprets, and synthesizes during decision making.[26] Because strategic decisions are complex and of major significance to an organization, achieving high-quality decisions requires the incorporation of as much relevant information as possible, as well as appropriate and creative ways of combining this information.[27]

Most prominently in this research stream, Hambrick and Mason argued in their upper-echelons theory that important sources of differences come from TMT members' values, cognitions, and personalities.[28] Empirical studies have confirmed this reasoning: Diversity in TMT members' cognitive backgrounds, as well as TMT interaction processes in which task-related differences in information and opinions are openly discussed, enhances strategic decision quality.[29] This logic has mainly been used for describing the processes within the TMT, just as I did in chapter 2.

The logic of information-processing theory suggests that the quality of strategic decisions will be higher when middle managers' information is successfully incorporated into strategy formulation because middle managers' information is likely to be markedly different from that of the TMT.[30] This difference stems from the different sources of information that middle managers have access to through their organizational function, as well as the different schemes with which they interpret organizational events.[31]

Based on this reasoning, we have reasoned that "information exchange" is one of the key processes in the interface. A good information exchange (I will later describe when an information exchange can be seen as "good") is a way to ensure high-quality strategic decisions as well as high-quality implementation. Information exchange is a two-way process between the TMT and middle managers that consists of asking for (party A), giving (B), and reviewing (A and B) information, where A and B can be either TMT members or middle managers.

Mutual Influencing

There is also a second interface process, which relates to the way in which decisions are implemented by middle managers. Strategy implementation has been less well researched than strategy formulation, but different perspectives do exist on how to achieve successful implementation.[32] In the context of interface between TMT and middle managers, the "interpersonal process view" is particularly informative.

The interpersonal process view of strategy implementation emphasizes that communication and interaction processes between the actors involved in strategy implementation are essential for success.[33] The emerging research stream on strategy processes and practices proposes that strategy is primarily a matter of actions and interactions between organizational actors[34] and confirms the logic of the interpersonal process view.

Scholars who have built on the interpersonal process view have suggested that TMTs exert influence on middle managers to generate commitment to and understanding of the strategy.[35] Furthermore, TMTs aim to install in middle managers a strong sense of organizational recognition, individual ownership, and motivation for decision implementation, as this facilitates implementation of the strategy.[36]

Middle manager research has emphasized that middle managers also influence the TMT. Their goal is often to receive resources for implementation, have their input taken into account, and get new ideas accepted.[37] Furthermore, middle managers may attempt to influence which issues enter the strategic agenda or direct the TMT to their course of strategic action.[38] Thus the TMT and middle managers are involved in a myriad of influence processes toward each other.

Based on this reasoning, we have concluded in our research that during the episodes of interaction a mutual influencing process takes place between the TMT and middle managers. We have defined *mutual influencing* as a two-way process between the TMT and middle managers that consists of an attempt to influence (A), articulation of a reaction to the influence attempt (B), and negotiation of the influence attempt (A and B) with the purpose of balancing forces for stability and change. Again, A and B can be either TMT members or middle managers. Both the TMT and middle managers may initiate influence cycles, and both can be influenced as a result of an influence attempt by the other.

Managing Information Exchange and Mutual Influencing

To manage the processes of information exchange and mutual influencing, TMTs should strive for high levels of cognitive flexibility during the information exchange process and integrative bargaining during the mutual influencing process. I will now discuss cognitive flexibility and integrative bargaining in more detail.

Cognitive Flexibility

The theory of information processing suggests that with the complexity and multidimensionality of strategic decisions, the discrepant information from the TMT and middle managers, based on their organizational functions and perspectives, should increase decision quality.[39] However, for this discrepant information to be beneficial, it must be made explicit in the interactions between the TMT and middle managers during the episodes of contact and each party must accept and be willing to understand it.

In the field of communication studies, researchers have used the term *cognitive flexibility* to describe group members' awareness of various possible options for dealing with a situation, a willingness concerning adaptation and flexibility in new situations, and the ability to represent knowledge from different conceptual and case perspectives.[40] The construct of cognitive flexibility is particularly relevant in the context of the TMT–middle manager interface because it captures the extent to which group members collectively interpret their environment and how they process information that contains conflicting elements.

Integrating information processing theory and the terminology of communication research, we propose that the extent to which a process of information exchange between TMT and middle managers is effective depends on the cognitive flexibility in the process. Adapting the original definition to the interface, we have defined *cognitive flexibility* as the extent to which the information exchange process between the TMT and middle managers is characterized by reflecting, reviewing information, taking different perspectives, being open to hearing from each other, being able to change opinions, and developing a large variety of interpretations.

When cognitive flexibility is high, the interaction between the TMT and middle managers is characterized by reflecting, reviewing, perspective taking, openness, respect, and changing of opinions. When cognitive flexibility is low—that is, when there is cognitive rigidity—TMT members and middle managers tend to stick to their own perspectives, neglect what the other party says, are unwilling to change perspectives, and possibly even show disrespect toward the other party.

Cognitive flexibility during the TMT–middle manager information exchange process will benefit high-quality decisions through several different mechanisms. First, when cognitive flexibility is high, more and more diverse information is taken into account. Decision processes benefit from including extensive and comprehensive information, even when a high speed of decision making is also required,[41] because they lead to more complete and balanced decisions.

Second, when cognitive flexibility is high, the complexities of the cause-and-effect relationships inherent in the strategy process will be better understood. Since strategic decision processes are typically characterized by novelty, complexity, and open-endedness,[42] high cognitive flexibility allows the TMT and middle managers to make accurate sense of the information obtained from the environment.

Finally, cognitive flexibility will increase the creativity with which information is interpreted and the alternatives that are generated, which may induce "cognitive shifts" in interpretation that facilitate change.[43] The TMT and middle managers can achieve cognitive flexibility during information exchange by explicitly asking for information, providing both solicited and unsolicited information, and critically reviewing the information.

It is not self-evident that the TMT and middle managers engage in extensively asking for and giving information, nor is it self-evident that they critically review the information received. A great deal of information comes to the TMT via formalized organizational systems. This situation may decrease the TMT's perception that it needs to explicitly ask for information from middle managers because TMT members may assume that they have all the needed information, even when this is not the case.[44]

For their part, middle managers may be reluctant to share information and engage in a critical discussion when they fear negative consequences for their organizational positions or when they see little chance for acceptance of their ideas.[45] Prior research has suggested that power differences, such as those between the TMT and middle managers, inhibit the open sharing of information. Less powerful members engage in self-censorship, and more powerful members withhold information to protect and increase their power.[46] Therefore, we expect that the degree to which the TMT and middle managers are able to achieve cognitive flexibility during the information exchange process will differentiate between a more or a less effective interface.

Integrative Bargaining

To capture the extent to which mutual influencing between the TMT and middle managers is successful, we build on the notion of integrative bargaining from the negotiations literature.[47] This work is particularly relevant to the interface of the TMT and middle managers because the asymmetry of information, influence, and interests between the two parties resembles a multiparty, mixed-motive negotiation rather than a collaborative problem-solving process.[48]

Integrative bargaining in the interface model describes the degree to which the mutual influencing process between the TMT and middle managers is characterized by finding common or complementary interests that benefit both parties rather than just one.[49] When integrative bargaining is high, the mutual influencing processes of the TMT and middle managers will be oriented toward achieving a win-win situation. In contrast, when integrative bargaining is low, the mutual influencing process is characterized by a win-lose dynamic in which the parties act as adversaries, each protecting its own fixed position or point of view.

Integrative bargaining implies a way of dealing with opposing interests between the TMT and middle managers that is cooperative and by which value for both parties is created.[50] In the context of strategic decision making and implementation, such an interchange implies that both the TMT and middle managers can influence each other in pushing for continuation of the current strategy versus engaging in new strategic initiatives.

We expect that integrative bargaining is positively related to implementation quality for several reasons. First, we expect that integrative bargaining will improve decision implementation through increased commitment of middle managers to strategy implementation. Since integrative bargaining takes the interests of both parties equally seriously, middle managers will be more likely to perceive an alignment between their interests and the final strategic decision, and this perception will increase their commitment to and motivation for implementation.[51]

In contrast, when integrative bargaining is low, TMT and middle managers may suppress or trivialize issues and evade dialectical interactions.[52] In such a situation, middle managers' reactions are likely to include a sort of compliance by which they superficially support a given strategy but do not generate high levels of effort to actually execute it because they do not see their interests represented.[53]

Second, we expect that integrative bargaining will benefit decision implementation, given that the TMT should make better decisions for resource allocation in the implementation process. Because middle managers often have better and more realistic insights into what effective implementation entails, and because integrative bargaining results in middle managers' input being taken into account, high integrative bargaining should result in a better allocation of resources than low integrative bargaining.[54]

Third, we expect that integrative bargaining will benefit implementation quality through increased creativity of the generated solutions and ideas. Given the different interests and perspectives of the TMT and middle managers, achieving win-win solutions through integrative bargaining is difficult and most likely involves the redefinition of initially incompatible standpoints.[55] Therefore, achieving solutions that result in this win-win dynamic will require more creativity than would achieving solutions that are based solely on the interests of the TMT or middle managers.

Interaction Moments: Windows of Opportunity

Cognitive flexibility and integrative bargaining are important for formulating high-quality strategic decisions and successfully implementing them. But how do you achieve that when you work, as most TMTs and middle managers do, under severe time pressure with only limited opportunities to interact with each other?

Most of the existing research has implicitly assumed that there is ample opportunity for the TMT and middle managers to interact. But the starting point of our model is the opposite: We propose that opportunities for contact between the TMT and middle managers are relatively short and infrequent because of the heavy time restrictions imposed on their contact. This implies that both parties are well advised to know how to use these windows of opportunity.

A first point in this matter is to accept the scarcity of contact as a defining element of the TMT–middle manager relationship. Thus, over time, the relationship between the TMT and middle managers is characterized by episodes of contact and periods during which there is no contact. Contact may take place face-to-face, by phone, through written communication, and so on and occur between at least one TMT member and one middle manager. It may be formal, for example, by scheduled meetings with fixed agendas and protocols, or informal, through phone calls and spontaneous encounters in hallways or before meetings.[56]

When the moments of direct contact are characterized by a high level of cognitive flexibility and integrative bargaining, the interface works well. These characteristics ensure effective information exchange and mutual influencing processes that contribute to the quality of strategic decisions and the success of implementation. However, the moments of contact have an additional function: They serve to coordinate and adapt the behavior of each party for the periods in which there is no contact.

Ensuring Alignment With Limited and Infrequent Interaction

How can you as a TMT ensure that the middle managers do what you want when they are executing the strategy within the organization? And how can you as a middle manager make sure that the TMT takes into account your interests when making strategic decisions? The answer is that you cannot. But by exhibiting certain behaviors, you can at least increase your chances. I will now outline which behaviors can significantly increase the chances of alignment in the TMT and middle managers' actions, even without many opportunities for direct interaction.

Benefits of TMT Participative Leadership

For understanding how the TMT and middle managers influence each other without direct contact and with only limited possibilities for control, the notion of risk is central. An important aspect of the risk to the TMT is whether to rely on middle managers' information as a basis for strategy formulation and to allocate resources to initiatives proposed by middle managers. The extent to which the TMT allows this risk in its relationship with middle managers is related to the TMT's "participative" versus "self-sufficient" leadership approach.

TMT participative leadership can be defined as TMT behaviors that seek middle managers' input in the process of strategy formulation.[57] Participative leadership implies that the TMT puts a high value on middle managers' information, seeks frequent interaction with middle managers to obtain this information, and uses middle managers' information as a basis for strategy formulation.

With such participative leadership, the TMT acts based on the understanding that the TMT and middle managers each have a valuable, albeit distinct, contribution to make to the strategy process. Prior research has indicated that TMTs that seek the input of experienced executives make not only better but also faster strategic choices.[58]

In contrast, if TMT leadership is low in participation and high in self-sufficiency, the TMT does not put value on middle managers' input for strategy formulation, uses the interaction with middle managers to inform them about decisions that have been made rather than asking for input, and relies on its own information for strategy formulation. In this situation, the TMT acts with the understanding that the TMT, rather than middle managers, has access to strategy-relevant information.

We propose that TMT participative leadership is positively related to cognitive flexibility and integrative bargaining during the interface processes. Thus we suggest that the behavior of one party, here the TMT, influences the system of interactions between the TMT and middle managers because TMT behavior elicits particular reactions from middle managers. There are several reasons we expect this effect to take place.

First, exercising TMT participative leadership implies that the TMT acknowledges the inherent interdependencies between the TMT and middle managers and is willing to take the risk of relying on middle managers' perspectives. When the TMT demonstrates such openness to middle managers, middle managers are likely to react by providing more information and taking themselves seriously as partners in strategy formulation. This perception will induce cognitive flexibility in the TMT–middle manager information exchange because both partners will then be willing to hear each other's perspective, critically review information, and change existing opinions.

This mode of interaction will also stimulate integrative bargaining in the mutual influencing process, as both parties are willing to explore each other's interests and cooperate to create mutual value. In contrast, when TMT role behavior is self-sufficient, the TMT ignores its inherent dependency on middle managers for strategy formulation, which is likely to lead to cognitive rigidity and a low level of integrative bargaining since the TMT does not see a value in engaging in those processes.

Second, with high participative leadership, the TMT will seek more interaction with middle managers and the number of episodes of contact should increase. Since cognitive flexibility is a collective capability residing in the interaction of the TMT and middle managers, and since the development of such collective capabilities is enhanced by repeated interactions over time,[59] more rather than fewer interaction episodes will increase the development of such collective capabilities. Similarly, integrative bargaining is enhanced through extensive interactions that build collective capabilities and understandings.[60]

Finally, participative leadership will also improve the ways in which the interaction episodes are used. As the episodes of contact provide relatively rare windows of opportunity for the TMT and middle managers, they should be used well to achieve favorable outcomes. Since participative TMTs are likely to stimulate critical debate and are active in asking for information and reacting to middle managers' input, TMT and middle managers' interaction is likely to be more focused on achieving collective outcomes rather than wasting time on formal procedures and political behavior. Such interaction will stimulate cognitive flexibility and prevent rigidity.[61]

TMT participative leadership should also enhance integrative bargaining because it helps both parties explore the various interests underlying their positions and unravels the criteria that embody the playing field on which an integrative course of action can be found. Furthermore, it enhances the creativity needed to find integrative solutions.

The Importance of Middle Managers' Active Engagement

Middle manager active engagement is the extent to which middle managers are interested in, actively involved in thinking about, and proactively engaged in behaviors that can contribute to strategy formulation and implementation.[62] When middle manager active engagement is high, middle managers see themselves as having an important role in strategy formation and regularly seek interaction with the TMT to provide input.

For example, prior research into the context of middle managers from subsidiaries gaining attention from TMT members at headquarters has outlined that middle managers can be more or less active in terms of exercising voice, taking initiatives, and building a profile.[63] Similarly, a recent study described how middle managers "established close contact with the senior manager to continuously present and negotiate new concepts and procedures."[64]

In contrast, when middle managers are low in active engagement, they see themselves as passive executors of the decisions the TMT makes, do not seek much interaction with the TMT, and instead focus on their own activities, such as those of their own business unit, rather than participating in strategy formation.[65]

We propose that middle manager active engagement will positively relate to the interface processes' cognitive flexibility and integrative bargaining. Similar to our reasoning on the effects of TMT participative leadership, we thus suggest that the behavior of one party, here the middle managers, shapes characteristics of the interactions between the TMT and middle managers. We expect that this effect takes place for several reasons.

First, when middle managers are interested in strategy formulation and implementation, they are likely to contribute more information during their interactions with the TMT because they see the relevance of such contributions for positive organizational outcomes.[66] This situation will increase cognitive flexibility because it enables the TMT and middle managers to have a more detailed and elaborate view of current circumstances, which stimulates creative thinking. More extensive information will also promote integrative bargaining because the availability of information facilitates the integration of different perspectives in finding win-win solutions.[67]

Second, when middle managers are actively engaged, they will also be more motivated to discuss and review information that the TMT brings in. This engagement will contribute to cognitive flexibility because middle managers' motivation to understand the TMT's perspective induces a constructive debate and changing of opinions without the fear of "losing face." Middle managers' increased motivation to discuss and review information will also contribute to integrative bargaining because they are more focused on achieving strategy outcomes that serve the organization as a whole rather than solely their own interests.

Finally, middle managers who are actively engaged are likely to be more constructively critical toward strategy, which will lead to a more extensive discussion and careful consideration of alternatives.[68] This situation should increase cognitive flexibility because critical discussions demand the synthesis of diverse perspectives.[69] It should also promote integrative bargaining because middle managers' constructively critical attitudes should lead to more persistence in their influence attempts toward the TMT and hence more creativity in finding solutions.

The Role of Trust

In chapter 2, I discussed the benefits of high trust among TMT members for the TMT's internal processes. Trust also plays a key role in the relationship between the TMT and middle managers. Specifically, the extent to which the TMT shows participative leadership and middle managers show active engagement depends on their trust in each other.

When the TMT trusts middle managers to implement the TMT's decisions in accordance with the TMT's intent and trusts that middle managers' input in strategy formation reflects an organization-wide rather than a private interest, the TMT will perceive an incentive for being more vulnerable toward middle managers because it sees great benefits in including middle managers in its strategy formulation processes. In this situation, the TMT will develop more TMT participative leadership.

Participative leadership increases vulnerability because it reduces the control that the TMT has on the outcomes of strategic decision making and hence increases the chance of middle managers misusing their increased power.[70] In contrast, when the TMT has low trust in middle managers, they tend to engage in less risk-taking behavior—that is, less TMT participative leadership—because the TMT will perceive little benefit in including middle managers' information and a high chance of middle managers' misusing their power. Therefore, the TMT is less likely to create a position in which it becomes vulnerable toward middle managers.

When middle managers have so much trust in the TMT that the TMT takes into account their information for strategy formulation and provides them with resources for strategy implementation, middle managers will also have higher incentives for interacting with the TMT. That is, they will see the episodes of contact with the TMT as important ways of ensuring resources and providing strategic input and will likely seek that interaction with the TMT more often and engage in it more actively. Hence middle managers will show more active engagement because they are willing to be more vulnerable toward the TMT. Middle manager active engagement implies vulnerability because middle managers' engagements provide the TMT with the chance to misuse middle managers' information and input.

In contrast, when middle managers have less trust in the TMT, they will perceive the interaction with the TMT as a symbolic ritual rather than as an opportunity to exert influence. This perception will decrease their willingness to be vulnerable because they see little benefit in providing the TMT with information and a high chance that the TMT may misuse that information. Hence middle managers will show less active engagement.

Outside the Boardroom: Concluding Remarks

With the interface model, we wanted to show how the TMT and middle managers can create alignment in the absence of many interaction moments. Since the relationship between these two parties is characterized by asymmetries of information, interests, and influence, it is not self-evident that such alignment exists. And if the alignment is not there, it is not easy to build or repair.

The notions of cognitive flexibility and integrative bargaining, as characteristics of successful interaction, provide two concrete starting points from which to work on alignment. In addition, TMT participative leadership and middle manager active engagement are behavioral styles that each party separately can start using that increase the chances of achieving successful interaction.

Make It Work for Your TMT

1. How would you describe the interface between the TMT and middle managers in your organization?
2. When are the moments of contact between the TMT and middle managers? Are they formal or informal, planned or spontaneous, short or long? Do you use them effectively?
3. To what extent is cognitive flexibility apparent during information exchanges between the TMT and middle managers? How could you increase it?
4. To what extent is the mutual influencing process between the TMT and middle managers characterized by integrative bargaining? What could you do to increase it?
5. How strong is the TMT's trust of the middle managers? How well do you think the middle managers trust the TMT?

CHAPTER 4

TMT Sensemaking About Middle Managers

What happens in the boardroom when a top management team (TMT) discusses strategy and makes decisions on how to implement it? And how does a TMT, in practice, deal with questions of how to lead the organization's middle managers? These questions were the starting point of an in-depth 6-month case study of one TMT, which was reported in *Small Group Research* in 2007.[1] In this chapter, I describe the methods and results of this study in a condensed form and discuss how it is relevant for other TMTs. The aim of this chapter is to illustrate the processes within the TMT that can influence how it deals with middle managers.

In the case study, our research team studied the TMT of a Dutch organization with about 3,000 employees. Through observing 23 of the TMT's meetings, performing a series of in-depth interviews with individual TMT members, and having full access to all organizational documents, we were able to obtain relatively complete information on the way in which this TMT made sense of its leadership task toward middle managers.

The Leadership Challenge

The relationship between the TMT and middle managers is in essence a leader-follower relationship. Leadership can be described as an influencing process where leaders influence others to understand and agree about what needs to be done and how to do it. Strategic leadership, more specifically, designates leadership at the top of organizations. Researchers have described it as consisting of strategic, relational, and symbolic aspects that take place between leaders, such as the TMT, and immediate followers, such as middle managers.[2]

Most of the TMT research so far has focused on the "strategic" aspect of TMT leadership. It has paid less attention to the relational aspects of leadership.[3] The relational aspect of strategic leadership, on the other hand, has been extensively studied at the level of the individual CEO, but researchers have not discussed what this implies for TMTs. This research does illustrate, however, that relational aspects of top leadership are key for ensuring decision implementation and organizational performance.

TMT researchers have mainly focused on intra-TMT factors, such as the team's composition or decision-making process, and have studied how these factors relate to organizational performance.[4] With this strong internal focus, it seems almost as if upper-echelons research has conceived of the TMT as an independent, not to say omnipotent, entity that directly influences organizational performance without any intermediary process. Realists, or those with senior executive experience, might find this all the more surprising, as the political reality within organizations clearly shows how much TMTs depend on middle managers.[5]

As I outlined in detail in chapter 3, managing the interface with middle managers can be considered an important aspect of the TMT task because of the catalytic role that middle managers play in the implementation of strategic decisions.[6] Middle managers are important for creating alignment in organizations, and they influence organizational performance.[7]

Middle managers are also able to redirect strategies, delay implementation, reduce the quality of implementation, and sometimes even sabotage it.[8] This can occur in situations where middle managers' self-interest is at stake, when they perceive the new strategy as flawed, or when they are incapable of implementing it.[9] Thus, to be effective, top managers have to find ways to gain middle managers' commitment or at least their compliance, as I described in detail in chapter 3.

Sensemaking About Leading Middle Managers

Strategic leadership on the TMT level implies that the process of influencing others to achieve shared objectives is carried out by more than one person. Thus TMT leadership contains an extra, collective dimension as compared with leadership on the individual-CEO level. TMT members have to coordinate and align their individual ideas and actions to develop a common understanding of their leadership approach that they carry out collectively. However, our research team observed that few studies have reported how TMT members understand this leadership aspect of their task. To understand and describe how leadership issues play a role in TMT interaction, we use the concept of sensemaking.

Sensemaking is a process through which individuals make sense of uncertainties in the environment through interaction with others.[10] This way, they negotiate among themselves an acceptable account of what is going on. This process of interpreting events to create meaning is triggered by perceptions that events are somehow ambiguous, surprising, or confusing.[11] Because TMTs must comprehend a great deal of vague, ambiguous, and often conflicting information from many sources,[12] including information related to middle managers, we considered sensemaking to be an adequate concept to capture characteristics of TMT interaction about leading middle managers.

Sensemaking is intimately connected to action. Action both precedes interpretation and meaning giving and follows it. Weick[13] has used the concept of enactment to describe the phenomenon that when people act according to what they perceive, they construct parts of their environment. Thus sensemaking is an iterative process of meaning giving and enactment.[14] Moreover, characteristics of the sensemaking process are consequential for the actions that follow.[15] Sensemaking is also adaptive over time as truths of the moment change, develop, and take shape.[16]

Researchers have studied TMT sensemaking during strategic change,[17] in the context of shared cognitions about strategy,[18] and in terms of the interpretative ambiguity that results from cognitive diversity.[19] However, TMT sensemaking about leadership, to our knowledge, has never been addressed in previous research. Therefore, one of the main objectives of our case study was to address the following research question: What is the content of TMT sensemaking about leading middle managers, and how can this be expected to influence decision implementation?

Case Illustration: The Research Setting

We studied the TMT of a Dutch organization, which operates in the public domain, using a longitudinal case study design[20] with a 6-month period of observation. We inferred our focal process of interest, TMT sensemaking, from observations collected during the weekly meetings as well as from interviews with the individual TMT members. We promised anonymity for the organization as a condition for reporting, so we refer to the studied organization as Alpha.

Alpha has about 3,000 employees. The organization can best be characterized as a professional bureaucracy, which implies that Alpha relies, in its structural configuration, on the skills and knowledge of its operating professionals.[21] This structure is common in general hospitals, educational institutions, public accounting firms, social work agencies, and some production firms.[22] The environment in which the organization operated during the research period can be characterized as rather turbulent: Government regulations for the industry in which the organization operated were subject to major changes that affected the choice of appropriate strategies with which to survive the turbulence.

The executive board of this organization was a TMT consisting of three members: the president, the vice president, and the chief operating officer (COO). All were male and roughly around the age of 50. Although this may seem to be a very small TMT given the size of the organization, the size of this TMT is not uncommon in the Netherlands. Previous research on the top 30 companies in the Netherlands (which have an average number of employees about 10 times larger than Alpha) indicated that even in these companies, the average TMT size is five.[23]

In this TMT, only the COO had reached his current position through a career within the organization. The other members had entered from outside. This TMT operated as an organizational entity and could, therefore, be studied as an intact team. The TMT reported to the supervisory board of the organization. Although the president had the final responsibility, the team functioned on a basis of equality.

The tasks of the TMT at Alpha, as stated in official organizational sources, can be described as having the final responsibility for the policy of the organization, including appointing key personnel, taking the initiative for major organizational changes (e.g., growth and restructuring), and managing finances and centralized staff functions. At the beginning of the observational period, the team members had been working together for about 1 year. The president was mainly responsible for the external contacts of the organization, the vice president for finance and human resource management, and the COO for the internal operations of the organization.

Middle managers in Alpha were responsible for divisions of the organization. Within the limits of general rules and procedures, these divisions operated with considerable autonomy. Middle managers formed the link between the TMT and their operational divisions, having to combine demands from the top and from the bottom. Based on our detailed observations during the meetings, as well as extensive interviews with the individual TMT members and company documents, we analyzed TMT sensemaking about middle managers.[24] In the following section, I describe the results of these analyses.

Images of Leadership in the TMT

Unity in Actions

During a series of in-depth interviews, all TMT members talked about several aspects of their relationship with middle managers. First, they mentioned the importance of TMT unity in actions toward middle managers. For example, the president noted the importance of consistency in action among TMT members: "Everyone should do the same things in every situation. Otherwise, if you don't operate as a team, middle managers play off the TMT members against each other."

Along the same line, the vice president pointed out, "If your employees get the impression that if you say 'turn left,' it can easily be 'right,' because another TMT member might say that, your decisions will not be readily implemented." The vice president also described an example of a situation where he got the impression that the president had said things to middle managers that were contrary to what the TMT had decided earlier. His reaction was to immediately confront the president with his impressions, indicating the importance he put on unity in actions by the TMT.

Second, it became clear that all TMT members perceived decision implementation through middle managers as an important, yet sometimes problematic, TMT task. For example, the COO noted, "Decision implementation is often a problem in Alpha. When middle managers don't want something, it is just not going to happen." As the best way to handle this, he stated, "Therefore, it is so important to keep on massaging things and have many bilateral consultations, in order to achieve legitimization for your decisions." He specifically advocated influencing people through one-to-one contacts as compared with formal meetings with all the middle managers.

The president mentioned a desire for more power sharing between the TMT and middle managers. He would like to work with all middle managers on the TMT level: "This way, your decisions will be broadly based, which is beneficial for decision implementation. Now middle managers perceive themselves as each others' competitors."

The interviews also dealt with various other topics, such as the advantage of having a TMT in place instead of a single manager for dividing tasks: "You can sometimes make a few adjustments to the various roles of the TMT members. If, for example, one member can't deal with a certain middle manager too well, you could switch certain issues and tasks around." Furthermore, the COO mentioned, "The TMT has too much on the agenda and actually should make more room to include the people around us."

Despite the limited number of episodes in this analysis for making detailed analyses, it seems that leading middle managers was a topic that was on the minds of the TMT members. Furthermore, the importance of decision implementation through middle managers was mentioned by all TMT members, who also advocated TMT unity in actions toward middle managers for achieving this.

The importance of such unity in action for a TMT is intuitively appealing: To successfully lead middle managers, TMT members should be consistent in their actions and act as one to the outside world. Yet this intuitive logic has not been reflected in scientific knowledge on teams. As outlined before, TMT researchers have mainly focused on factors inside the team or external to the organization[25] and seldom on the relationship between the TMT and lower echelons.

Research on nonmanagerial teams also has mainly focused on internal team factors,[26] and when external activities have been taken into account,[27] a detailed analysis of how team members coordinate their actions toward others is missing. Some indication of the importance of such a construct exists in Jarzabkowski and Searle's concept of TMT collective action,[28] but they, too, neglect the relationship between the TMT and others.

Although relatively absent in research, the notion seemed important for the TMT we studied. Therefore, our research team coined the term *TMT unity in actions* to designate the process whereby TMT members coordinate their actions toward others in such a way that the team is perceived by others as a unified whole. In the results of the analysis of TMT interaction during the meetings, the importance of TMT unity in actions will be emphasized once more.

Images of Middle Managers

During their weekly board meetings, the TMT expressed different types of images of middle managers. We distilled three different types of images: generalized images of middle managers as a barrier to decision implementation, images of idiosyncrasies of specific middle managers, and images of middle managers as strategic organizational elements. We found these images to be particularly interesting as they provide information about the TMT's implicit theories on how to lead middle managers.

Sensemaking of middle managers as a barrier to decision implementation often occurred as a means to explain why decision implementation did not go as the TMT members would have liked. Thus it is not surprising that when the TMT members talked about the middle managers as a group, they were rather critical and perceived the middle managers' behavior as resistance toward TMT initiatives.

A metaphor that appeared repeatedly clearly illustrates this perceived resistance—namely, the image of the middle managers as people who "dig their heels in" as a reaction to TMT initiatives. The president was the first to use it in Meeting 2 in the context of a new project that was launched by the TMT: "When you propose something that is entirely within the scope of your responsibility, then they dig their heels in." In later meetings, the metaphor was mentioned again by the COO and by the head of the strategy department when the TMT members were reflecting on past events and issues that did not go as well as they had expected. Moreover, the TMT assumed that the middle managers felt that they "always had to come running up" and that they had a "deeply rooted distrust" of the TMT.

Thus the TMT, in making sense of middle managers' perceived behavior, referred to middle managers as one group to understand why decision implementation in Alpha did not always go exactly as the members would have liked. This observation is in line with the fact that sensemaking occurs whenever the current state of the world is perceived to be different from the expected state of the world,[29] which was also the case for this TMT. Talking about the middle managers in a generalized way implies that the TMT members saw the cause of the middle managers' resistance more in the middle managers' position in the organization than in the middle managers personally. This can be illustrated by the COO's bringing up the proposition that middle managers are "torn" or "caught in the middle" between the TMT and their organizational units.

In addition to talking about middle managers as a group, the TMT discussed the *idiosyncrasies of specific middle managers*. In talking about specific middle managers, the TMT discussed possible intentions, emotions, and behaviors of the middle managers, for example, saying that a middle manager "did not operate sensibly" or "was disappointed." Where the images of middle managers as a barrier to decision implementation were mostly generalized across time and situations, images of individual managers were more closely linked to certain situations or persons at a specific time. For example, when the TMT wanted a middle manager who "did not operate sensibly" to be kept within the organization during earlier discussions, members stated that they were willing to let him go later, should that prove more beneficial to the organization as a whole.

Talking about individual middle managers focused TMT members' attention on the human side of these managers as people whose behavior, cognitions, and emotions were at issue. Sometimes this was triggered by negative evaluations of a middle manager. In another case, when the TMT member perceived a middle manager to be disappointed with a certain issue, he specifically stated that he had to "manage his expectations" because he wanted to keep that middle manager within the organization. Focusing on middle managers as individuals during sensemaking can thus lead to tailored actions from which decision implementation could benefit.

TMT members also discussed the function of the middle managers as a *strategic organizational element.* For example, when a new middle manager had to be appointed, TMT members discussed the specific requirements for the new appointment. Working on their vision for the organization, they expressed that it would be beneficial to appoint a middle manager with certain characteristics as well as to design the middle manager's organizational function in a certain way.

Furthermore, they discussed the future middle manager position after the restructuring of an organizational unit. In this process, some middle managers were perceived to be afraid that their level of responsibilities and involvement in power relations would be reduced to an unacceptable level. The TMT members discussed their need to make clear to these middle managers that they did not want this to happen. Discussing middle managers as strategic organizational elements allowed the TMT to, once in a while, rethink the position of middle managers in the organization. For example, the TMT considered changing the middle manager position and the specific contents and requirements of the job, if necessary, to adjust to a current or future situation.

Self-Image of the TMT

In addition to the TMT's images of the middle managers, our analysis showed references to its self-image. TMT members discussed their identity as a TMT with regard to their leadership role, addressing questions such as, "Who are we as a TMT? What should we do as a TMT? Where do we want to go in future?" In doing so, TMT members made sense of their tasks and roles vis-à-vis middle managers. For example, they stated that the TMT's task is to "establish contacts, give them the tools, and then pass the ball to the different departments."

A metaphor that was often used and is representative of the content of this category is that the TMT is supposed "to pull the wagon." This implies the idea that if the TMT does not move the organizational wagon, no one will do it. Combined with the analysis of the interviews, the self-image of the TMT seems to center on being a group of hardworking people trying to pull everyone in the organization forward. This is considered to be necessary, as the TMT sees the environment as changing in ways that middle managers sometimes do not.

Combining the TMT Self-Image With Images of Middle Managers

The TMT members rarely made explicit references to a specific leadership approach. However, their dominant ideas about leadership are evident from the images they exchanged. The images of the middle managers and the TMT self-image imply views on how to best lead middle managers. The main metaphors used—the wagon that the TMT wants to pull and the middle managers who dig their heels in—suggest a relationship of two opposing forces in which the TMT keeps on pulling and the middle managers resist.

Several times, the TMT members expressed their wish to be supported by middle managers in pulling the organizational wagon. In the absence of this happening, the TMT members thought they had to take the lead, boosted by their self-image as "three people with a tendency to control." Their orientation to control is further illustrated by their remarks that they "do not want to hand over control."

These images of having to take the lead and wanting to be in control point to a preference for a directive leadership approach. When discussing the idiosyncrasies of specific middle managers, the TMT referred to a father-child type of relationship. For example, TMT members noted that a middle manager "is getting himself into trouble, and we have to get him out of it" or that "we should have a firm talk with these organizational units." This exemplifies a paternalistic leadership notion.

It is interesting that TMT sensemaking about leadership also included discussing what members thought might be the leadership style preferred by the middle managers. For example, they assumed that middle managers found it an ideal situation when the TMT was on vacation, which was pointed out during the meetings as well as in the interviews. Contrary to the TMT's own preferences of rather directive and paternalistic leadership approaches, members assumed that the middle managers wanted a more laissez-faire type of leadership.

These assumptions about the middle managers' preferred leadership approaches are also in line with the perceived resistance from middle managers and the expression that middle managers have a "deeply rooted distrust" toward the TMT. The discrepancy between the TMT's images of leadership (directive, paternalistic) and the leadership model the TMT assumed to be desired by middle managers (laissez-faire) was an important trigger for TMT leadership being a recurrent theme in the meetings and formed the need for continued sensemaking.

Thus it appears from our observations of the TMT meetings as well as from the interviews that the TMT members exchanged images of middle managers and themselves to construct shared images that helped them to make sense of their leadership role. They did not explicitly discuss these images. Usually, a certain image would be mentioned by a TMT member in the first place, after which the expressed image (e.g., the corrective father-child notion or the directive idea of the wagon that has to be pulled forward) was readily accepted by the other team members. When analyzing the observations over time, we saw not only that certain ideas were proposed and evolved into shared images but also that certain images reappeared at later moments. Thus we noted a tendency among TMT members to invoke established images to make sense of ongoing events.

It is interesting to note that we did not observe changes in images of the middle managers or the TMT itself, nor did we see indications of changes in the leadership role. Yet we would think that such changes might occur in situations that can no longer be explained by the established images. Sticking to such images might be counterproductive, especially in situations of change or crisis.[30] This focuses attention on the question of how the TMT responds to discrepant information.

In the current study, we saw that TMT members noted some discrepancy between how the TNT led and what middle managers would have preferred but did not use this information to adapt their views and leadership approach. We saw the COO more often referring to what he assumed to be the desired leadership style of middle managers (laissez-faire) than the others did. The other members seemed to trust his perspective given his internal career and used the perceived discrepancy to insist on their own preferred leadership approach. To better understand the dynamics and implications of this process, we will first discuss the enactment part of the sensemaking process.

Action Planning and Reflection on Past Actions

A typical feature of sensemaking is its iterative nature with meaning giving and enactment. In analyzing episodes of TMT interaction that related to actions toward middle managers, we saw two temporal foci: planning for future actions toward middle managers and reflecting about past actions and their results.

Concerning action planning, one conclusion stands out as the most clear: In the view of the TMT, action toward the middle managers often necessitates talking. Conversations with middle managers were prepared in detail during TMT meetings. The TMT discussed the goal of the conversation, the tone of it, and sometimes the specific division of roles, which points at the importance of coordinating future actions toward middle managers, labeled earlier as TMT unity in actions. That is, to everyone outside the TMT (including middle managers), it should be clear that the TMT is unified in its ideas and plans. Even though discussions take place within the boardroom, none of that should be visible externally.

Other action planning units involved writing memos or, on a more complex and abstract level, designing evaluation and incentive systems. In these episodes, action planning included a focus on developing standards with which organizational units could be evaluated and to which incentives could be linked. The prevalence of this type of action planning increased over the course of the observational period. This course of action was mainly triggered by the TMT's images of middle managers as a barrier to decision implementation and thoughts about how to overcome resistance and motivate middle managers to achieve decision implementation. Several times, TMT members expressed a wish to use more incentives, a transactional leadership notion, with which they hoped to gain middle managers' support.

The TMT not only planned future actions but also reflected on past actions. Reflections were on past actions or behavior of the TMT itself ("I don't think we have endless discussions"; "Shouldn't we have done more here?"), their expectations for middle managers ("Maybe we should not expect this from them"), and how they had approached middle managers in certain issues ("We have presented that as a possibility, which is different from . . ."). Reflecting about past actions was regularly followed by expressing intentions for the future in terms of planning to communicate better and making things more clear.

In both action categories, we saw the emphasis on direct contact and unity in actions as being the TMT's generic leadership approach. The *directive leadership* image came back in the team's preference for explaining and imposing as compared to listening when preparing its meetings with middle managers. The paternalistic image was reflected in subtleties, such as when talking about the tone of voice that would be used in meetings with middle managers. Furthermore, the intention to install incentive structures and evaluation mechanisms as a means to direct and correct suggests an image of *transactional leadership* as an effective way to achieve decision implementation.

These observations regarding the enactment part of the sensemaking cycle confirm the view that emerged from the analysis of the TMT's images. The TMT appears to act in accordance with the image it holds of its leadership role. Reflecting on the results of its actions, the TMT confirms the images of the middle managers and of itself, deciding to persist in the leadership approach associated with it. Again, looking for trends over time, we were not able to perceive any changes. Discrepant information, in particular about middle managers resisting the approach, seemed to strengthen the earlier adopted patterns of meaning and associated action rather than to change it.

TMT Sensemaking About Leadership

On the basis of the foregoing, our research team could answer the first part of the research question ("What is the content of TMT sensemaking about leading middle managers?"). As I have illustrated in this chapter, sensemaking about leadership contains three elements: (a) images of followers and their leadership expectations, (b) self-image and preferred leadership approaches, and (c) the relationship between the two as a basis for action.

Consistent with the view on leadership as a relational activity,[31] TMT sensemaking includes elements from both sides of this relationship: the middle managers and the TMT. The category of action is indicative of the fact that meaning giving and action are closely linked in an iterative sequence.[32] The presence of the TMT self-image as a category illustrates that identity construction is a basic function of sensemaking.[33]

Our analysis revealed clear links between these categories—between the images of middle managers and the self-image, between the two temporal foci for action, and between the images and action categories—suggesting that they form a coherent set of ideas that can be understood as the TMT's understanding about its leadership role. We also found that the categories were reiterated over time, with images and actions confirming each other, and that there was a strong agreement between TMT members that was maintained over time. In some cases, we could observe how an image proposed by an individual member was accepted and upheld by the TMT as a whole. Furthermore, the TMT's preference for directive and transactional leadership was also reflected in its actions, even when the results of its actions were not as the members had desired.

The second part of the research question ("How can this be expected to influence decision implementation?") can be answered only partially, as our observations did not extend to the actual process of decision implementation in the organization. Confining ourselves to what did and did not happen in the TMT, there are two points to make. First, sensemaking as a process of gaining a shared understanding enables the TMT to "speak with one voice," which can enhance the effectiveness of its interaction with the middle managers. The importance of such TMT unity in actions toward middle managers was also advocated in the interviews and was put into practice when the TMT prepared meetings with middle managers by coordinating and clarifying in detail how it would act.

Second, we have noted a clear self-confirming tendency in the sensemaking process. The TMT's views and preferred actions remained the same during the 6-month observation period, even though middle managers were perceived to be resisting its decisions. Occasional discrepant information, showing that the approach taken had limited success, resulted in opting for "more of the same"—that is, "talking more" and "explaining even better"—rather than changing views in a new sensemaking effort.

It is also interesting to note that as far as we are aware, the images of the middle managers—and those of the TMT itself—were never discussed in contacts with those middle managers. This points at the closed nature of the images, which prevents them from being adjusted in the case of a poor fit. What this implies for decision implementation can only be inferred.

Although TMT unity in action might be seen as an antecedent of effective decision implementation and achieving shared understandings through sensemaking might contribute to this, a self-confirmatory pattern of sensemaking may pose a risk when maintained over a longer period of time. There is an extensive body of literature about the need for vigilant information processing and renewed sensemaking for continuous learning and adapting.[34] The theory of organizational learning[35] makes similar points.

These general notions also apply to the TMT and its relationship with the middle managers. If the TMT fails to pick up signs of discrepant information from the side of middle managers, decision implementation is most likely to suffer. Given the powerful role of the middle managers, as mentioned by Currie and Procter and Floyd and Wooldridge,[36] one would expect that self-confirmatory sensemaking will undermine decision implementation in the long run.

TMT Sensemaking: Concluding Remarks

The starting point of the study reported in this chapter was to find evidence for TMT sensemaking about leading middle managers while enriching TMT research with a qualitative account of a TMT in action. Transcripts of TMT meetings and interviews were analyzed to see how a TMT made sense of its leadership task toward middle managers. This has resulted in several key constructs: images of leadership during TMT sensemaking (directive, transactional, paternalistic), characteristics of the sensemaking process (self-confirmatory), and TMT unity in action as determinant of decision implementation.

The results indicated that TMT sensemaking was organized along one dimension for understanding middle managers' behavior, one for understanding its self-image in relation to middle managers, and one related to the enactment of its understandings. By considering sensemaking as an iterative process, we concluded that sensemaking in the TMT that we studied could be seen as self-confirmatory: The TMT expressed an image about leading middle managers, enacted this image, and persisted in its approach, even when it encountered discrepancies between its images and those of middle managers.

The importance of TMT unity in actions was emphasized as a key success factor for leadership at the TMT level. Thus it seems that sensemaking can be seen as a process that facilitates the development of shared understandings, yet when such sensemaking leads to self-confirming cycles, decision implementation is likely to suffer.

Make It Work for Your TMT

1. To what extent does your TMT show a clear unity of actions?
2. How do you think middle managers perceive TMT unity of actions?
3. Which images of middle managers are present in your TMT?
4. How do they help or hinder the relationship between the TMT and middle managers?

CHAPTER 5

Middle Manager Perspectives

What do middle managers find important in their top management team (TMT)? And how do they evaluate their TMT on those dimensions? These questions were the starting point of a large-scale investigation of middle managers' perspectives in different countries.[1] In this chapter, I report some of the findings of this study. Thus, to complement chapter 4, in which the TMT's perspective on middle managers was described, this chapter provides insight into the side of middle managers.

Insight into middle managers' perspectives of their TMT is particularly relevant for TMTs, as such perspectives will often shape middle managers' behavior toward the TMT. The way in which middle managers think and feel about the TMT influences the extent to which they spend time and energy on fully achieving the TMT's goals; hence the effectiveness with which the TMT can reach its goals is dependent on middle managers' perspectives on the TMT.

In our study, we asked middle managers for their perceptions of the TMT's performance. We asked two questions: What do you expect from your TMT's performance, and how do you evaluate the actual performance of the TMT in your current organization? Interestingly, we observed clear discrepancies between those two aspects.

Why Study Middle Managers' Expectations and Evaluations of TMT Performance?

The idea for this study was based on our observation that relatively little is known about middle managers' perceptions of their TMT. This is true despite the fact that research on leadership effectiveness in general has pointed at the interest in followers' perspectives of their leaders.[2] Researchers using stakeholder theory have also emphasized the relevance of assessing stakeholders' perspectives of top managers.

Stakeholders have the power to give or withhold resources, such as information, materials, and their own efforts. They are therefore critical for the TMT to achieve its objectives.[3] Although TMTs of course have a variety of stakeholders both inside and outside the organization, researchers have identified middle managers as a particularly relevant group, as middle managers are central in both strategy formulation and implementation.[4]

We focus on the topic of TMT performance, as it provides a clear reference point for middle managers' evaluations. Most researchers within the TMT literature have focused on the overall success of the organization to indicate TMT performance, as achieving organizational performance can be seen as the ultimate responsibility of the TMT.[5] Organizational performance is then typically assessed with accounting indicators.[6] These measures provide aggregated performance information and have the advantage of being easily accessible and supposedly objective.[7] Yet using this as the sole criterion for TMT performance has drawbacks.

A first drawback is that organizational performance is influenced by many factors not directly related to TMT activities, among which are competitors' behavior, the business environment, and even luck. This can make it problematic to attribute the current success, or failure, of an organization purely to the TMT's actions. A second drawback is that the TMT's effects on organizational performance are likely to crystallize only after some time lag, which makes it problematic to use this criterion as an indicator for current TMT performance. Finally, since the work of a TMT consists of many different tasks and responsibilities, it is quite likely that TMTs vary in the success with which they complete various aspects of their work. Thus using organizational performance as the sole criterion neglects the inherent multidimensional nature of TMT performance.

Our knowledge of dimensions of TMT performance may therefore contribute to developing "early-warning systems" for TMT malfunctioning and prevent such malfunctioning from translating into severe consequences for organizational performance at a later stage. With our study, we thus wanted to contribute not only to insight into middle managers' perspectives but also to the discussion on what constitutes good TMT performance.

Five Aspects of TMT Performance

Based on a thorough review of the literature relating to TMTs, nonmanagerial teams, and organizational effectiveness, we identified five areas of TMT performance.

Company Results

As pointed out earlier, company results is the dominant TMT performance area used in prior TMT research.[8] Top managers have the responsibility to guard shareholder interests and lead their companies in a financially sound way. Their incentive pay arrangements are often linked to company results.[9] Therefore, it seems likely that company results are a salient TMT performance area not only for shareholders but also for other stakeholder groups such as middle managers.

Strategic Leadership

The TMT's main duty is to make strategic decisions and implement these through leadership actions, with the aim of contributing to the overall success of the organization.[10] Strategic leadership activities comprise, for example, creating and communicating a vision for the future, making decisions that improve the competitive position, developing organizational structures, and managing multiple constituencies.[11]

Connectedness

This aspect represents the extent to which the TMT develops and maintains relationships to other intra- and extraorganizational actors.[12] It is an essential part of top managers' work to be connected to others in their environment, both inside and outside their organization.[13] Therefore, the quality, quantity, and diversity of the contacts and network of the TMT are proposed to be aspects of its performance.[14]

TMT Unity

TMT unity is the degree to which TMT members coordinate their actions toward others in such a way that the TMT is perceived by others as a unified whole, as I described in chapter 4 of this book. This aspect builds on other related constructs, such as TMT behavioral integration[15] and TMT collective action,[16] but extends these by adding a focus on how the TMT is perceived by others. That is, we suppose that TMT unity is an aspect that is visible for intraorganizational stakeholders, such as middle managers, and provides them with important cues of how successful the TMT is in aligning, promoting, and implementing new ideas.

Moral Leadership

In the light of recent scandals and unresolved world challenges, the topics of corporate social responsibility and moral leadership have been widely discussed in academic and popular literature.[17] Moral leadership can be described as the alignment between a TMT's words and deeds while leading others[18] combined with honesty and adherence to moral principles.[19] Moral leadership inspires commitment among followers[20] and positively affects a company's external reputation.[21] We therefore suggest that it is a salient performance area for middle managers when evaluating TMTs.

Research Focus

We were interested in two types of cognitions from middle managers: their expectations and their evaluations. Expectations are cognitive structures that an individual can hold about future activities and are, in an organizational setting, often associated with the occupancy of a certain organizational role.[22] Evaluations are also cognitive structures, but they have a focus on past activities instead of future ones and capture middle managers' subjective assessments of actual behavior of the TMT. The actions of top managers, because these managers are authority figures who are highly visible in their roles at the top of their organizations, are particularly prone to be the focal concept of evaluative processes of subordinates.[23]

In the empirical part of this study, we were interested to see whether middle managers' expectations and evaluations could be organized along the five dimensions of TMT performance that we have identified. We assumed that such expectations and evaluations are important not only because they influence middle managers' readiness to execute the TMT's decisions but also because they can influence the attitudes and behavior of middle managers' subordinates toward the TMT, the decisions of the TMT, and even the organization as a whole.

Collecting the Data

Our sample consisted of 108 French and 143 Dutch middle managers. This sample was drawn from the client pool of an international consultancy firm that included organizations from various industries and countries. In the context of the firm's annual research among its clients, all middle managers in the pool were invited to answer a web-based questionnaire on TMT performance. The questionnaire was available in four languages: English, German, French, and Dutch. In total, 2,430 e-mails were delivered to respondents in 19 countries, and 530 filled questionnaires were returned, of which 251 were usable for our purpose.

More than three-quarters of the respondents were male. The majority worked in either the secondary (i.e., manufacturing, chemical, energy, information technology, telecom) or the tertiary sector (i.e., service, media, leisure). They came from 152 different organizations of various sizes with a maximum of 8 respondents from the same organization. Middle managers' work experience ranged from fewer than 5 to more than 20 years.

Measuring Middle Managers' Expectations and Evaluations

We wanted to assess middle managers' expectations and evaluations of the five areas of TMT performance: company results, strategic leadership, connectedness, TMT unity, and moral leadership. Given the fact that TMT performance to our knowledge had never been assessed before from middle managers' perspectives, we developed new scales to capture the TMT performance aspects.

To formulate items that captured the theoretical domain of interest while also reflecting the practical reality of TMT work, we complemented the construct definitions of prior research with a series of interviews with managers and human resources (HR) professionals. Based on existing literature and the interview results, we developed three to five questions to capture the performance aspects. I report examples of these items here to give some insight into what we asked the middle managers in our study.

An example of an item for the company results aspect is "The company achieves outstanding financial results"; for strategic leadership, "The TMT has a clear vision of the company's future"; for connectedness, "The TMT is well-connected to important players inside the company"; for TMT unity, "The TMT speaks with one voice"; and for moral leadership, "The TMT brings into practice what it preaches."

To measure middle managers' expectations, we then asked them the following question: "Suppose you were asked to judge whether the top management team of your company effectively performs its task. Which criteria would you consider important to make this judgment?" They were asked to indicate on a 5-point scale, with scale anchors 1 = totally disagree and 5 = totally agree, the extent to which they agreed with the statement that "a top management team effectively performs its task if [text item]." To measure middle managers' evaluations of their TMTs' performance, we asked them to indicate on a 5-point scale, with scale anchors 1 = totally disagree and 5 = totally agree, to what extent they agreed with the statement that "the top management team of my organization [text item]."

We also asked middle managers to report any aspect of TMT performance that we had missed in the list of items. Analyses of the answers to this open question did not give indications that we had missed an important aspect. We also measured some characteristics of middle managers, such as their gender and years of work experience. Additionally, we asked them for the number of TMT members in their organization, the number of employees in their organization, and the sector in which they were working.

Analyses

In a series of factor analyses, we tested if the five performance areas were actually confirmed by our data. This turned out to be the case, although we removed some questions so that the dimensions formed a more coherent set of items. We also assessed if there were statistical differences between the two countries in terms of the structure of the performance areas. This was not the case; we interpreted this as an indication that the existence of the performance areas was valid across the different countries.

We then summarized the scores of the middle managers for their expectations and evaluations on each of the performance areas. We thereafter inspected the means and standard deviations of the performance dimensions and performed multivariate analyses of variance to see if individual and organizational variables were related to differences in the expectations and evaluations of the performance dimensions and if differences existed between countries.

Our analyses indicated that middle managers' expectations on the various dimensions of TMT performance were not significantly related to their gender, their work experience, the size of their TMT or organization, or the country in which they worked. Also for the evaluations, no significant multivariate effects were found. Thus middle managers' expectations and evaluations were similar in structure across countries, sectors of operation, middle managers' gender and work experience, and TMT and organizational size.

We also assessed to what extent middle managers' expectations and evaluations could really be seen as separate constructs. After all, it is not unlikely that one's expectations color the evaluations and vice versa. To address this concern, we first calculated the correlations between middle managers' expectations and evaluations on all performance dimensions. If the correlation between middle managers' expectations and evaluations of, for example, moral leadership were high, we would conclude that these two types of cognitions are related and that it might be difficult to make a distinction between them. If the correlations were low, this would indicate that they were separate constructs and that it would be meaningful to assess if discrepancies existed between middle managers' scores on the expectations and evaluations.

The results of these analyses show that the correlations between the evaluations and expectations on the same performance dimension were very low to moderate. Thus although the underlying dimensionality of TMT performance is similar for middle managers' expectations and evaluations of TMT performance, the two types of cognitions do represent different and almost uncorrelated constructs.

Results of the Study

Middle Managers' Expectations of Their TMT

To get an insight as to whether the scores of the middle managers on the various dimensions differed from each other, we performed t-tests between every pair of dimensions. Middle managers' expectations were highest for the dimensions of moral leadership (score 4.32) and strategic leadership (score 4.27), and these two dimensions did not significantly differ from each other. We found TMT unity (score 4.05) to be significantly less important and connectedness (score 3.92) again significantly less important than unity. Connectedness and company results (score 3.90) did not differ from each other. These results can also be seen in Table 5.1.

Middle Managers' Evaluations of Their TMT

We repeated the same procedure for middle managers' evaluations. Here, there are only two ranks: Company results (score 3.38), strategic leadership (score 3.37), and connectedness (score 3.37) scored highest and did not significantly differ from each other. Middle managers evaluated their TMT lowest on moral leadership (score 3.27) and TMT unity (score 3.20), and these dimensions did not differ significantly. These results also are reported in Table 5.1.

Discrepancies Between Expectations and Evaluations

The order of the dimensions is not identical for the expectations and evaluations. Particularly interesting in this ranking is the reverse order of

Table 5.1. Expectations and Evaluations of Middle Managers

Expectations			Evaluations		
Rank	Dimension	Score	Rank	Dimension	Score
1	Moral leadership	4.32	1	Company results	3.38
1	Strategic leadership	4.27	1	Strategic leadership	3.37
2	TMT unity	4.05	1	Connectedness	3.37
3	Connectedness	3.92	2	Moral leadership	3.27
3	Company results	3.90	2	TMT unity	3.20

company results and moral leadership across the two types of cognitions. While middle managers have the highest expectations for TMT moral leadership and strategic leadership and the lowest for company results and connectedness, they evaluate TMTs highest on company results and lowest on moral leadership and TMT unity. Thus discrepancies are particularly apparent on the dimensions of moral leadership and company results but less so on the other three dimensions.

As I mentioned before, it can be expected that middle managers' expectations and evaluations are based on the same underlying "feeling" that middle managers have about their TMT. However, through our statistical analyses, we could rule out this possibility. We therefore concluded that the two types of cognitions can clearly be seen as separate constructs: expectations with a focus on the future and evaluations with a focus on past TMT performance.

How TMTs Can Use These Results

The Five Performance Areas

Researchers who have focused on the performance of individuals, nonmanagerial teams, and organizations have long conceptualized performance as a multidimensional construct.[24] No such model existed for TMT performance. Yet, based on the complexity and multidimensionality of the TMT task, we reasoned that TMT performance also should be conceptualized as a multidimensional construct.

Our study revealed the existence of five relevant performance aspects. By measuring these dimensions and by testing them in exploratory and confirmatory factor analyses, we have established a model for evaluating TMT performance that goes beyond financial indicators. Although our main interest was in the stakeholder group of middle managers, this instrument might be used by other stakeholders as well, provided that they are close enough to the TMT to observe outcomes of the TMT's work.

Knowledge of the multiple dimensions of TMT performance can assist TMTs and supervisory boards in closely monitoring TMT impact. Since the outcomes of TMT work are more closely related to TMT than to organizational performance[25] and a positive relationship between

TMT and organizational performance exists,[26] the timely monitoring of TMT performance can function as an early indicator for subsequent effects on the organizational level. This can also be of interest to trainers and coaches who work with TMTs to improve their work both for goal setting and for examining the effects of their interventions.

The Perspectives of Middle Managers

The five performance dimensions can also be used to explore in more detail the expectations and evaluations that middle managers have of their TMT. Since leadership effectiveness models and implicit leadership theories have been shown to be consequential for individual and organizational outcomes,[27] insight into the contents, determinants, and consequences of such models is certainly valuable for TMTs.

Insight into middle managers' expectations and evaluations may also be a starting point for assessing the actual relationship between the TMT and middle managers. For example, one could ask how the amount and type of communication from the TMT toward middle managers are related to middle managers' perceptions of TMT moral leadership or if the degree to which the TMT is coordinating its actions toward middle managers is related to company performance.

TMT unity might be particularly interesting in this respect, as almost no prior research has considered this aspect of TMT leadership. Since most of the studies on leadership expectations and evaluations have investigated individual-level leadership,[28] a dimension of TMT unity, which exists only on the team level, was never an issue.

The results of the study reported in this chapter showed that TMT unity is a separate dimension of TMT performance, which middle managers in both France and the Netherlands found important. Thus, to successfully perform its tasks, it is important that the TMT is acting as one unit that is consistent across time and situations in communicating its decisions and that middle managers perceive the TMT to act as such.

The observed discrepancy between middle managers' high expectations of TMT moral leadership and their relatively low evaluations of it is also noteworthy. This finding relates to other research findings, as the relevance of moral leadership and perceptions of integrity of management have been illustrated before.[29] This work has shown that employees' perceptions of top management integrity are positively related to satisfaction, commitment, and organizational citizenship behavior and negatively to intentions to quit their job.[30]

In contrast, perceptions of nonintegrity have been related to reduced TMT credibility, employees' disenchantment,[31] reduced support,[32] and counterproductive behavior.[33] Given our results on discrepancies and prior research on the potential effects of such discrepancies, more research is clearly warranted to further explore the determinants and consequences of middle managers' cognitions on moral leadership.

Middle Manager Perspectives: Concluding Remarks

The results of this study provide TMTs with knowledge about middle managers' expectations concerning top managerial performance. Researchers have argued before that leaders should enhance their knowledge about the performance expectations of their subordinates.[34] This is important for TMTs as well, as they face demands from different stakeholder groups and these stakeholders make decisions to give or withhold resources that are required for organizational performance.[35] Yet research has shown that many senior executives fail to recognize the importance of others' perceptions for their own reputations.[36]

Moreover, the outward appearance of TMTs and stakeholder uneasiness with TMT deterioration have been shown as part of the downward spiral of large corporate bankruptcies.[37] Middle managers' emphasis on moral leadership might be particularly noteworthy in this respect, as previous research—albeit not on middle managers specifically—has shown that organizations where employees see managers as practicing what they preach experience higher organizational commitment, customer satisfaction, and financial performance.[38]

Make It Work for Your TMT

1. How does your TMT perform on each of the five performance areas—company results, strategic leadership, connectedness, TMT unity, and moral leadership?

2. How do you think middle managers see your performance in these areas?

3. Would you expect that there are discrepancies between what middle managers expect from the TMT and what they observe in practice?

CHAPTER 6

Making It Work

A top management team (TMT) matters for its organization, right? At the end of this book, I hope to have made clear that this is indeed the case. The way in which a TMT makes this impact relates to factors inside the boardroom and factors outside the boardroom. Inside the boardroom, the TMT's interpersonal processes and states are particularly relevant for achieving high-quality decisions. And outside the boardroom, the way in which the TMT deals with middle managers determines the success of decision implementation. In this last chapter, I will recap the essentials of the previous chapters.

Inside the Boardroom

In chapter 2, I described characteristics of the TMT's internal processes and states. Over the past 20 years, researchers have gained increased understanding of how the behavior of TMT members relates to important organizational outcomes. Most researchers have focused on outcomes that relate to (a) the quality of the TMT's decisions, (b) the way the TMT performs as a group, and (c) the performance of the organization as a whole. Based on a thorough analysis of the available literature, some clear recommendations can be given to TMTs in practice.

First, disagreement and discussions among the TMT members during decision making are to be stimulated. Such processes, also called "task conflict," lead to better decisions because they incorporate the diverse knowledge and expertise of the different TMT members. TMTs can stimulate task conflict by explicitly asking for different opinions, promoting extensive discussions, and not coming to a consensus too early.

In these discussions, it is important that a spillover effect from task to relationship conflict is avoided. Relationship conflicts are disagreements that relate to people with animosities and interpersonal fights. Because it is all too easy to misinterpret a purely task-related discussion as an attack on the person, the two types of conflict are often closely related. One way to decrease the chances that such spillover effects occur is to craft a state of high trust in the TMT. When TMT members trust each other, they tend to give each other the benefit of the doubt and retain a focus on the team's common goals and task.

Another aspect of the TMT's internal dynamics is the extent to which members function as a behaviorally integrated team rather than as a fragmented group of "semi-autonomous barons." Behavioral integration describes the extent to which a TMT makes joint decisions, openly shares information and opinions, and carries out the work collectively. Although some researchers have expressed doubts about whether this is at all possible, or necessary, for TMTs, the research on behavioral integration clearly shows that working as a team is related to better outcomes.

To achieve the beneficial effects of task conflict and behavioral integration, it is not necessary to have a very high frequency of communication. Researchers have shown that more frequent communication within the TMT is not related to better outcomes. It seems that successful TMTs manage to use each interaction opportunity particularly well. TMTs that are less successful, paradoxically, need more interaction moments—taking time and energy away from their other activities—and are not more successful even with them.

In the analysis of the literature, it also became clear that the TMT's interaction processes and states—even when they exhibit all the beneficial characteristics—do not always directly translate into better organizational performance. The TMT's strategic decisions and the way TMT members function as a group clearly benefit, but apparently something more needs to happen to also achieve high performance for the organization as a whole. Based on this observation, I proposed that this "something" relates to the subsequent implementation of the TMT's strategic decisions and the way in which the TMT works with middle managers to achieve a high quality of implementation.

Outside the Boardroom

Outside the boardroom, the TMT works with middle managers to implement strategic decisions. In chapter 3, I described the recently developed "interface model." This model can help TMTs in thinking about how to deal with middle managers. Using this model, I described why it is important to achieve cognitive flexibility and integrative bargaining in the interaction between the TMT and middle managers. TMTs can stimulate this beneficial type of interaction by using a participative leadership style. Middle managers can stimulate it by being actively engaged.

In chapter 4, I described how a TMT understood and coordinated its leadership task toward middle managers. I based this chapter on an in-depth analysis of the weekly board meetings of a Dutch TMT of a medium-sized organization. By closely inspecting the dynamics of this TMT and subsequently linking them to the current literature, a picture arose of the necessity for TMTs to inspect the images they have of middle managers.

It is through constructing images that a TMT can understand its leadership approach. But we also concluded in this study that these images tend to be relatively fixed even where adaptation may be useful, for example, when decision implementation is not going well. Thus it seems useful for TMTs to every now and then reflect on the underlying assumptions and interpretations with which they approach middle managers. This may not only lead to more insight about the sensemaking processes within the TMT but also provide starting points for decision implementation with middle managers.

In chapter 5, I described middle managers' side of the interface and specifically the expectations they have about TMT performance and their evaluations of it. In the reported study, there were five performance dimensions along which we could organize middle managers' perspectives: company results, strategic leadership, connectedness, TMT unity, and moral leadership. Because TMT performance can be seen as an inherently multidimensional construct, the specification of these five dimensions may be helpful for TMTs to get a grasp on the success with which they perform the various aspects of their work.

It became clear that discrepancies often exist between what middle managers find important and how they evaluate their TMT on it. The dimensions of company results and moral leadership were particularly interesting in this respect. Middle managers found company results a relatively unimportant aspect of TMT performance but evaluated their TMT to perform well on it. On the other hand, middle managers have high expectations for the TMT's moral leadership but find that their own TMT does not perform too well. Such discrepancies can have implications for middle managers' commitment and motivation and would thus be worthwhile to explore and take seriously as a TMT.

All in all, I hope this book has provided insight for TMTs, and those around them, on how they can make a positive impact on their organizations. Focusing on the TMT's internal processes and states and its way of dealing with middle managers are two domains to start from in making a TMT work.

Notes

Chapter 1

1. Certo et al. (2006); Hambrick (2007).
2. Cohen and Bailey (1997); O'Toole et al. (2002); Wagemanet al. (2008).
3. Hambrick and Mason (1984).
4. Eisenhardt et al. (1997); Klenke (2003).
5. Edmondson et al. (2003); Forbes and Milliken (1999); Pettigrew (1992); Tengblad (2002).
6. Hambrick (1994; 2007).
7. Wageman et al. (2008).
8. Hackman (2002); Wageman et al. (2008).
9. Cohen and Bailey (1997); Wageman et al. (2008).
10. Wageman et al. (2008).
11. Guth and MacMillan (1986); Hambrick (1994).
12. Mintzberg (1983); Nutt (1986).
13. Edmondson et al. (2003); Hambrick (1994).
14. Ancona and Nadler (1989); Gibson and Schroeder (2003).
15. Cohen and Bailey (1997); O'Toole et al. (2002).
16. Ancona and Nadler (1989); Hambrick (1994).
17. Hackman (2002).
18. Edmondson et al. (2003); O'Toole et al. (2002).
19. Hambrick and Mason (1984); Janis (1982).
20. Amason and Mooney (1999).
21. Amason (1996); Korsgaard et al. (1995).
22. Smith et al. (1994); Tajfel and Turner (1986).
23. Janis (1982).
24. Collins and Clark (2003); Geletkanycz and Hambrick (1997).
25. Carpenter et al. (2004); Hambrick (2007); Hambrick and Mason (1984).
26. Haleblian and Finkelstein (1993); Leifer and Mills (1996).
27. Carpenter et al. (2004); Certo et al. (2006); Nielsen (2010).
28. Lawrence (1997); Priem et al. (1999).
29. Boal and Hooijberg (2000), p. 523.
30. Carpenter et al. (2004); Certo et al. (2006); Hambrick (2007); Nielsen (2010).

31. See, for example, Bales (1950); Hackman (1987); McGrath (1984); Steiner (1972); Tuckman (1965).

32. Marks et al. (2001); Smith et al. (1994).

33. Marks et al. (2001); Srivastava et al. (2006).

34. Carpenter et al. (2004); Peterson et al. (2003); Smith et al. (1994).

35. Dopson et al. (1992).

36. Floyd and Wooldridge (1997); Wooldridge et al. (2008).

37. Floyd and Wooldridge (1997); Guth and MacMillan (1986).

38. Gibson and Schroeder (2003); Sims (2003).

39. Floyd and Lane (2000).

Chapter 2

1. Roberto (2003); Tengblad (2006).

2. Edmondson et al. (2003).

3. De Dreu and Weingart (2003); Marks et al. (2001).

4. Dean and Sharfman (1996); Eisenhardt (1989b); Raes et al. (2011).

5. Edmondson et al. (2003); Hackman (2002).

6. Carmeli and Schaubroeck (2006).

7. Amason (1996); Dooley and Fryxell (1999); Leifer and Mills (1996).

8. Cyert and March (1963); Hambrick and Mason (1984); March and Simon (1958).

9. Edmondson et al. (2003); Olson et al. (2007).

10. Amason (1996); Dooley and Fryxell (1999); Olson et al. (2007); Simons et al. (1999).

11. Amason (1996); Dooley and Fryxell (1999); Olson et al. (2007).

12. Amason (1996); Dooley and Fryxell (1999); Olson et al. (2007).

13. Talaulicar et al. (2005).

14. Eisenhardt (1989b); Talaulicar et al. (2005).

15. Chen et al. (2005); Elron (1997).

16. Ensley and Pearce (2001); Ensley et al. (2007).

17. Barsade et al. (2000); Ensley and Pearce (2001); Ensley et al. (2002); Simons et al. (1999).

18. Nutt (1999).

19. Hickson et al. (2003); Nutt (1999).

20. Hambrick (1994; 1995).

21. O'Toole et al. (2002).

22. Carmeli and Schaubroeck (2006).

23. Carmeli (2008); Lubatkin et al. (2006).

24. Carmeli (2008).

25. Ling et al. (2008).

26. Ling and Kellermanns (2010); Smith et al. (1994).

27. Smith et al. (1994).

28. Ling and Kellermanns (2010).

29. Steiner (1972).

30. Smith et al. (1994).

31. Amason (1996); Janssen et al. (1999).

32. Ensley and Pearce (2001); Ensley et al. (2002).

33. Amason (1996); Barsade et al. (2000); Ensley and Pearce (2001); Ensley et al. (2002); Ensley et al. (2007).

34. De Dreu and Weingart (2003); Simons and Peterson (2000).

35. Barrick et al. (2007); Srivastava et al. (2006).

36. Elron (1997); Smith et al. (1994).

37. Burgers et al. (2009); Ensley et al. (2007); Lin and Shih (2008); Smith et al. (1994).

38. Janis (1982).

39. Elron (1997).

40. Lin and Shih (2008).

41. Smith et al. (1994).

42. Mayer et al. (1995); Schoorman et al. (2007).

43. Rau (2005).

44. Olson et al. (2007); Simons and Peterson (2000).

45. Simons and Peterson (2000).

Chapter 3

1. For a full report of this research, see Raes et al. (2011).

2. Geletkanycz and Hambrick (1997); Mintzberg (1973); Weick (1979).

3. Wooldridge et al. (2008).

4. Floyd and Wooldridge (1992b; 1997).

5. Floyd and Wooldridge (1997); Guth and MacMillan (1986).

6. Gibson and Schroeder (2003); Sims (2003).

7. Dirks and Ferrin (2002); Mayer and Gavin (2005).

8. Currie and Procter (2005); Floyd and Lane (2000); Floyd and Wooldridge (1997).

9. Currie and Procter (2005); Floyd and Wooldridge (1992b).

10. Dutton and Ashford (1993); Dutton et al. (1997); Dutton et al. (2001).

11. Wooldridge and Floyd (1990).

12. Wooldridge and Floyd (1990).

13. Collins and Clark (2003); Geletkanycz and Hambrick (1997).

14. Roberto (2003).

15. Balogun and Johnson (2004); Guth and MacMillan (1986).

16. Bouquet and Birkinshaw (2008a; 2008b); Dutton and Ashford (1993).

17. Balogun and Johnson (2004); Guth and MacMillan (1986); Ketokivi and Castaner (2004).

18. Eisenhardt (1989a).

19. Guth and MacMillan (1986); Ketokivi and Castaner (2004).

20. Sims (2003).

21. Eisenhardt (1989a).

22. Guth and MacMillan (1986).

23. Ancona (1989); Edmondson et al. (2003).

24. Cook (2005); Rousseau et al. (1998); Schoorman et al. (2007).

25. Mayer et al. (1995), p. 712.

26. Dooley and Fryxell (1999); Galbraith (1973); Tushman and Nadler (1978).

27. Eisenhardt (1989b); Hambrick and Mason (1984); Leifer and Mills (1996).

28. Hambrick and Mason (1984).

29. Amason (1996); Dooley and Fryxell (1999); Olson et al. (2007).

30. Martin and Eisenhardt (2010); Wooldridge et al. (2008).

31. Currie and Procter (2005); Dutton and Ashford (1993); Wooldridge et al. (2008).

32. Bourgeois and Brodwin (1984).

33. Cannella and Monroe (1997); Floyd and Wooldridge (1992a); Love et al. (2002).

34. Hoon (2007); Jarzabkowski and Spee (2009).

35. Floyd and Wooldridge (1992a); Hambrick and Cannella (1989); Noble (1999).

36. Amason (1996); Dooley and Fryxell (1999); Ketokivi and Castaner (2004).

37. Currie and Procter (2005); Floyd and Wooldridge (1997); Martin and Eisenhardt (2010).

38. Dutton and Ashford (1993); Dutton et al. (1997); Dutton et al. (2001).

39. Floyd and Wooldridge (1992a); Noble (1999).

40. Martin and Anderson (1998); Spiro et al. (1992).

41. Eisenhardt (1989b).

42. Edmondson et al. (2003); Mintzberg et al. (1976).

43. Foldy et al. (2008); Mom et al. (2007).

44. Roberto (2003).

45. Guth and MacMillan (1986); Schilit and Paine (1987).

46. Edmondson et al. (2003).

47. Floyd and Wooldridge (1992a); Hambrick and Cannella (1989); Noble (1999).

48. Edmondson et al. (2003).

49. Ury and Patton (1991); Walton and McKersie (1965).

50. Edmondson et al. (2003); Lax and Sebenius (1986); Walton and McKersie (1965).

51. Edmondson et al. (2003); Lax and Sebenius (1986); Walton and McKersie (1965).

52. Janssen et al. (1999).

53. Guth and MacMillan (1986).

54. Mantere (2008); Martin and Eisenhardt (2010).

55. Janssen et al. (1999).

56. Dutton and Ashford (1993); Hoon (2007).

57. Edmondson et al. (2003); Schilit and Paine (1987); Vroom and Yetton (1973).

58. Eisenhardt (1989b).

59. Rico et al. (2008); Waller et al. (2004).

60. Bacon and Blyton (2007).

61. Janis (1982).

62. cf. Kelley (1992).

63. Bouquet and Birkinshaw (2008a; 2008b).

64. Hoon (2007), p. 929.

65. Guth and MacMillan (1986).

66. Kelley (1992); Martin and Eisenhardt (2010).

67. Janssen et al. (1999).

68. Kelley (1992); Martin and Eisenhardt (2010).

69. Amason (1996).

70. Mayer et al. (1995); Mayer and Gavin (2005).

Chapter 4

1. Raes et al. (2007).

2. Vera and Crossan (2004).

3. Cannella and Monroe (1997).

4. Certo et al. (2006).

5. Balogun and Johnson (2004); Currie and Procter (2005).

6. Balogun and Johnson (2004).

7. Balogun and Johnson (2004); Currie and Procter (2005); Floyd and Wooldridge (1997).

8. Guth and MacMillan (1986).

9. Guth and MacMillan (1986).

10. Weick (1979; 1995).

11. Maitlis (2005).

12. Edmondson et al. (2003).

13. Weick (1995).

14. Weick et al. (2005).

15. Maitlis (2005).

16. Weick et al. (2005).

17. Gioia and Thomas (1996).

18. Knight et al. (1999).

19. Kilduff et al. (2000).

20. Yin (2003).

21. Mintzberg (1983).

22. Mintzberg (1983).

23. Glunk et al. (2001).

24. For a detailed description of the methods of data analysis, see Raes et al. (2007).

25. Carpenter et al. (2004).

26. Cohen and Bailey (1997).

27. For example, see Ancona and Caldwell (1992).

28. Jarzabkowski and Searle (2004).

29. Weick et al. (2005).

30. Weick (1979); Weick et al. (2005).

31. Vera and Crossan (2004).

32. Weick (1979).

33. Weick (1995).

34. Janis (1982); Weick et al. (2005).

35. Argyris (1999); Senge (1990).

36. Currie and Procter (2005); Floyd and Wooldridge (1997).

Chapter 5

1. For a full report of the study, see Glunk et al. (2007).

2. Hooijberg and Choi (2000).

3. Freeman and Reed (1983); Schneider (2002); Tsui et al. (1995).

4. Floyd and Wooldridge (1997); Raes et al. (2011).

5. Carpenter et al. (2004); Hambrick and Mason (1984).

6. Certo et al. (2006).

7. Cohen and Bailey (1997).

8. Carpenter et al. (2004); Certo et al. (2006); Hambrick and Mason (1984).

9. Carpenter and Sanders (2004).

10. Boal and Hooijberg (2000); Edmondson et al. (2003).

11. Boal and Hooijberg (2000).

12. Collins and Clark (2003).

13. Ancona and Nadler (1989).

14. Ancona and Nadler (1989); Collins and Clark (2003).

15. Hambrick (1994).

16. Jarzabkowski and Searle (2004).

17. Thomas et al. (2004).

18. Simons (2002a).

19. Treviño et al. (2000).
20. Cha and Edmondson (2006).
21. Treviño et al. (2000).
22. Katz and Kahn (1978).
23. Gibson and Schroeder (2003).
24. Cameron (1986); Cohen and Bailey (1997); Russell (2001).
25. Barrick et al. (2007).
26. Elron (1997).
27. Epitropaki and Martin (2005); Mayer and Gavin (2005).
28. Denison et al. (1995); Hooijberg and Choi (2000).
29. Mayer and Gavin (2005).
30. Mayer and Gavin (2005).
31. Cha and Edmondson (2006).
32. Tsui et al. (1995).
33. Mayer and Gavin (2005).
34. Hooijberg and Choi (2000); Tsui et al. (1995).
35. Tsui et al. (1995).
36. Treviño et al. (2000).
37. Hambrick and D'Aveni (1992).
38. Mayer and Gavin (2005); Simons (2002b).

References

Amason, A. C. (1996). Distinguishing the effects of functional and dysfunctional conflict on strategic decision making: Resolving a paradox for top management teams. *Academy of Management Journal, 39*(1), 123–148.

Amason, A. C., & Mooney, A. C. (1999). The effects of past performance on top management team conflict in strategic decision making. *International Journal of Conflict Management, 10*(4), 340–359.

Ancona, D. G. (1989). Top management teams: Preparing for the revolution. In J. Carroll (Ed.), *Social psychology in business organizations* (pp. 99–128). Hillsdale, NJ: Lawrence Erlbaum.

Ancona, D. G., & Caldwell, D. F. (1992). Bridging the boundary: External activity and performance in organizational teams. *Administrative Science Quarterly, 37*(4), 634–661.

Ancona, D. G. & Nadler, D.A. (1989). Top hats and executive tales: Designing the senior team. *Sloan Management Review*, 31(1), 19– 28.

Argyris, C. (1999). *On organizational learning*. Malden, MA: Blackwell.

Bacon, N., & Blyton, P. (2007). Conflict for mutual gains? *Journal of Management Studies, 44*(5), 814–834.

Bales, R. F. (1950). *Interaction process analysis: A method for the study of small groups*. Reading, MA: Addison-Wesley.

Balogun, J., & Johnson, G. (2004). Organizational restructuring and middle manager sensemaking. *Academy of Management Journal, 47*, 523–549.

Barrick, M. R., Bradley, B. H., Kristof-Brown, A. L., & Colbert, A. E. (2007). The moderating role of top management team interdependence: Implications for real teams and working groups. *Academy of Management Journal, 50*(3), 544–557.

Barsade, S. G., Ward, A. J., Turner, J. D. F., & Sonnenfeld, J. A. (2000). To your heart's content: A model of affective diversity in top management teams. *Administrative Science Quarterly, 45*(4), 802–836.

Boal, K. B., & Hooijberg, R. (2000). Strategic leadership research: Moving on. *Leadership Quarterly, 11*, 515–549.

Bouquet, C., & Birkinshaw, J. (2008a). Managing power in the multinational corporation: How low-power actors gain influence. *Journal of Management, 34*(3), 477–508.

Bouquet, C., & Birkinshaw, J. (2008b). Weight versus voice: How foreign subsidiaries gain attention from corporate headquarters. *Academy of Management Journal, 51*(3), 577–601.

Bourgeois, L. J., & Brodwin, D. R. (1984). Strategic implementation: Five approaches to an elusive phenomenon. *Strategic Management Journal, 5*(3), 241–264.

Burgers, J. H., Jansen, J. J. P., Van den Bosch, F. A. J., & Volberda, H. W. (2009). Structural differentiation and corporate venturing: The moderating role of formal and informal integration mechanisms. *Journal of Business Venturing, 24*(3), 206–220.

Cameron, K. S. (1986). Effectiveness as paradox: Consensus and conflict in conceptions of organizational effectiveness. *Management Science, 32*(5), 539–553.

Cannella, A. A., Jr., & Monroe, M. J. (1997). Contrasting perspectives on strategic leaders: Toward a more realistic view of top managers. *Journal of Management, 23*, 213–237.

Carmeli, A. (2008). Top management team behavioral integration and the performance of service organizations. *Group & Organization Management, 33*(6), 712–735.

Carmeli, A., & Schaubroeck, J. (2006). Top management team behavioral integration, decision quality, and organizational decline. *Leadership Quarterly, 17*(5), 441–453.

Carpenter, M. A., Geletkanycz, M. A., & Sanders, W. G. (2004). Upper echelons research revisited: Antecedents, elements, and consequences of top management team composition. *Journal of Management, 30*(6), 749–778.

Carpenter, M. A., & Sanders, W. G. (2004). The effects of top management team pay and firm internationalization on MNC performance. *Journal of Management, 30*(4), 509–528.

Certo, S. T., Lester, R. H., Dalton, C. M., & Dalton, D. R. (2006). Top management teams, strategy and financial performance: A meta-analytic examination. *Journal of Management Studies, 43*(4), 813–839.

Cha, S., & Edmondson, A. C. (2006). When values backfire: Leadership, attribution, and disenchantment in a values-driven organization. *Leadership Quarterly, 17*(1), 57–78.

Chen, G., Liu, C., & Tjosvold, D. (2005). Conflict management for effective top management teams and innovation in China. *Journal of Management Studies, 42*(2), 277–300.

Cohen, S. G., & Bailey, D. E. (1997). What makes team work: Group effectiveness research from the shop floor to the executive suite. *Journal of Management, 23*(3), 239–290.

Collins, C. J., & Clark, K. D. (2003). Strategic human resource practices, top management team social networks, and firm performance: The role of human resource practices in creating organizational competitive advantage. *Academy of Management Journal, 46*(6), 740–751.

Cook, K. S. (2005). Networks, norms, and trust: The social psychology of social capital. *Social Psychology Quarterly, 68*(1), 4–14.

Currie, G., & Procter, S. J. (2005). The antecedents of middle managers' strategic contribution: The case of a professional bureaucracy. *Journal of Management Studies, 42*(7), 1325–1356.

Cyert, R. M., & March, J. G. (1963). *A behavioral model of the firm.* Englewood Cliffs, NJ: Prentice Hall.

De Dreu, C. K. W., & Weingart, L. R. (2003). Task versus relationship conflict, team performance, and team member satisfaction: A meta-analysis. *Journal of Applied Psychology, 88*(4), 741–749.

Dean, J. W., & Sharfman, M. P. (1996). Does decision process matter? A study of strategic decision-making effectiveness. *Academy of Management Journal, 39*(2), 368–396.

Denison, D. R., Hooijberg, R., & Quinn, R. E. (1995). Paradox and performance: Toward a theory of behavioral complexity in managerial leadership. *Organization Science, 6*(5), 524–540.

Dirks, K. T., & Ferrin, D. L. (2002). Trust in leadership: Meta-analytic findings and implications for research and practice. *Journal of Applied Psychology, 87*(4), 611–628.

Dooley, R. S., & Fryxell, G. E. (1999). Attaining decision quality and commitment from dissent: The moderating effects of loyalty and competence in strategic decision-making teams. *Academy of Management Journal, 42*(4), 389–402.

Dopson, S., Risk, A., & Stewart, R. (1992). The changing role of the middle manager in the United Kingdom. *International Studies of Management and Organization, 22*(1), 40–53.

Dutton, J. E., & Ashford, S. J. (1993). Selling issues to top management. *Academy of Management Review, 18*(3), 397–428.

Dutton, J. E., Ashford, S. J., O'Neill, R. M., Hayes, E., & Wierba, E. E. (1997). Reading the wind: How middle managers assess the context for selling issues to top managers. *Strategic Management Journal, 18*(5), 407–423.

Dutton, J. E., Ashford, S. J., O'Neill, R. M., & Lawrence, K. A. (2001). Moves that matter: Issue selling and organizational change. *Academy of Management Journal, 44*(4), 716–736.

Edmondson, A. C., Roberto, M. A., & Watkins, M. D. (2003). A dynamic model of top management team effectiveness: Managing unstructured task streams. *Leadership Quarterly, 14*(3), 297–325.

Eisenhardt, K. M. (1989a). Agency theory: An assessment and review. *Academy of Management Review, 14*(1), 57–74.

Eisenhardt, K. M. (1989b). Making fast strategic decisions in high-velocity environments. *Academy of Management Journal, 32*(3), 543–576.

Eisenhardt, K. M., Kahwajy, J. L., & Bourgeois, L. J., III (1997). Conflict and strategic choice: How top management teams disagree. *California Management Review, 39*(2), 42–62.

Elron, E. (1997). Top management teams within multinational corporations: Effects of cultural heterogeneity. *Leadership Quarterly, 8*(4), 393–412.

Ensley, M. D., & Pearce, C. L. (2001). Shared cognition in top management teams: Implications for new venture performance. *Journal of Organizational Behavior, 22*(2), 145–160.

Ensley, M. D., Pearson, A. W., & Amason, A. C. (2002). Understanding the dynamics of new venture top management teams: Cohesion, conflict, and new venture performance. *Journal of Business Venturing, 17*(4), 365–386.

Ensley, M. D., Pearson, A. W., & Sardeshmukh, S. R. (2007). The negative consequences of pay dispersion in family and non-family top management teams: An exploratory analysis of new venture, high-growth firms. *Journal of Business Research, 60*(10), 1039–1047.

Epitropaki, O., & Martin, R. (2005). From ideal to real: A longitudinal study of the role of implicit leadership theories on leader-member exchanges and employee outcomes. *Journal of Applied Psychology, 90*(4), 659–676.

Floyd, S. W., & Lane, P. J. (2000). Strategizing throughout the organization: Managing role conflict in strategic renewal. *Academy of Management Review, 25*(1), 154–177.

Floyd, S. W., & Wooldridge, B. (1992a). Managing strategic consensus: The foundation of effective implementation. *Academy of Management Executive, 6*(4), 27–39.

Floyd, S. W., & Wooldridge, B. (1992b). Middle management involvement in strategy and its association with strategic type: A research note. *Strategic Management Journal, 13*(5), 153–167.

Floyd, S. W., & Wooldridge, B. (1997). Middle management's strategic influence and organizational performance. *Journal of Management Studies, 34*(3), 465–485.

Foldy, E. G., Goldman, L., & Ospina, S. (2008). Sensegiving and the role of cognitive shifts in the work of leadership. *The Leadership Quarterly, 19*(5), 514–529.

Forbes, D. P., & Milliken, F. J. (1999). Cognition and corporate governance: Understanding boards of directors as strategic decision-making groups. *Academy of Management Review, 24*(3), 489–505.

Freeman, R. E., & Reed, D. L. (1983). Stockholders and stakeholders: A new perspective on corporate governance. *California Management Review, 25*(3), 88–106.

Galbraith, J. R. (1973). *Designing complex organizations*. Reading, MA: Addison-Wesley.

Geletkanycz, M. A., & Hambrick, D. C. (1997). The external ties of top executives: Implications for strategic choice and performance. *Administrative Science Quarterly, 42*(4), 654–681.

Gibson, D. E., & Schroeder, S. J. (2003). Who ought to be blamed? The effects of organizational roles on blame and credit attributions. *International Journal of Conflict Management, 14*(2), 95–117.

Gioia, D. A., & Thomas, J. B. (1996). Identity, image, and issue interpretation: Sensemaking during strategic change in academia. *Administrative Science Quarterly, 41*(3), 370–403.

Glunk, U., Heijltjes, M. G., & Olie, R. (2001). Design characteristics and functioning of top management teams in Europe. *European Management Journal, 19*(3), 291–300.

Glunk, U., Raes, A. M. L., Heijltjes, M. G., & Roe, R. A. (2007). *Middle managers' perceptions of top management team performance: The crucial role of moral leadership*. Paper presented at Academy of Management annual meeting, Philadelphia, PA.

Guth, W. D., & MacMillan, I. C. (1986). Strategy implementation versus middle management self-interest. *Strategic Management Journal, 7*(4), 313–327.

Hackman, J. R. (1987). The design of work teams. In J. Lorsch (Ed.), *Handbook of organizational behavior* (pp. 315–342). Englewood Cliffs, NJ: Prentice Hall.

Hackman, J. R. (2002). *Leading teams: Setting the stage for great performances*. Boston, MA: Harvard Business School Press.

Haleblian, J., & Finkelstein, S. (1993). Top management team size, CEO dominance, and firm performance: The moderating roles of environmental turbulence and discretion. *Academy of Management Journal, 36*(4), 844–863.

Hambrick, D. C. (1994). Top management groups: A conceptual integration and reconsideration of the "team" label. Research in Organizational Behavior, 16, 171–213.

Hambrick, D. C. (1995). Fragmentation and the other problems CEOs have with their top management teams. *California Management Review, 37*(3), 110–127.

Hambrick, D. C. (2007). Upper echelons theory: An update. *Academy of Management Review, 32*(2), 334–343.

Hambrick, D. C., & Cannella, J. A. A. (1989). Strategy implementation as substance and selling. *Academy of Management Executive, 3*(4), 278–285.

Hambrick, D. C., & D'Aveni, R. A. (1992). Top team deterioration as a part of the downward spiral of large corporate bankruptcies. *Management Science, 38*(10), 1445–1466.

Hambrick, D. C., & Mason, P. A. (1984). Upper echelons: The organization as a reflection of its top managers. *Academy of Management Review, 9*(2), 193–206.

Hickson, D. J., Miller, S. J., & Wilson, D. C. (2003). Planned or prioritized? Two options in managing the implementation of strategic decisions. *Journal of Management Studies, 40*(7), 1803–1836.

Hooijberg, R., & Choi, J. (2000). Which leadership roles matter to whom? An examination of rater effects on perceptions of effectiveness. *Leadership Quarterly, 11*(3), 341–364.

Hoon, C. (2007). Committees as strategic practice: The role of strategic conversation in a public administration. *Human Relations, 60*(6), 921–952.

Janis, I. L. (1982). *Groupthink: Psychological studies of policy decisions and fiascos* (2nd ed.). Boston, MA: Houghton Mifflin.

Janssen, O., Van de Vliert, E., & Veenstra, C. (1999). How task and person conflict shape the role of positive interdependence in management teams. *Journal of Management, 25*(2), 117–141.

Jarzabkowski, P., & Searle, R. H. (2004). Harnessing diversity and collective action in the top management team. *Long Range Planning, 37*(5), 399–419.

Jarzabkowski, P., & Spee, A. P. (2009). Strategy-as-practice: A review and future directions for the field. *International Journal of Management Reviews, 11*(1), 69–95.

Katz, D., & Kahn, R. L. (1978). *The social psychology of organizations* (2nd ed.). New York, NY: John Wiley & Sons.

Kelley, R. E. (1992). *The power of followership: How to create leaders people want to follow and followers who lead themselves.* New York, NY: Doubleday/Currency.

Ketokivi, M., & Castaner, X. (2004). Strategic planning as an integrative device. *Administrative Science Quarterly, 49*(3), 337–365.

Kilduff, M., Angelmar, R., & Mehra, A. (2000). Top management-team diversity and firm performance: Examining the role of cognitions. *Organization Science, 11*(1), 21–34.

Klenke, K. (2003). Gender influences in decision-making processes in top management teams. *Management Decision, 41*(10), 1024–1034.

Knight, D., Pearce, C. L., Smith, K. G., Olian, J. D., Sims, H. P., Smith, K. A., et al. (1999). Top management team diversity, group process, and strategic consensus. *Strategic Management Journal, 20*(5), 445–465.

Korsgaard, M. A., Schweiger, D. M., & Sapienza, H. J. (1995). Building commitment, attachment, and trust in strategic decision-making teams: The role of procedural justice. *Academy of Management Journal, 38*(1), 60–84.

Lawrence, B. S. (1997). The black box of organizational demography. *Organization Science, 8*(1), 1–22.

Lax, D., & Sebenius, J. (1986). *The manager as negotiator: Bargaining for cooperation and competitive gain.* New York, NY: Free Press.

Leifer, R., & Mills, P. K. (1996). An information processing approach for deciding upon control strategies and reducing control loss in emerging organizations. *Journal of Management, 22*(1), 113–137.

Lin, H.-C., & Shih, C.-T. (2008). How executive SHRM system links to firm performance: The perspectives of upper echelon and competitive dynamics. *Journal of Management, 34*(5), 853–881.

Ling, Y., & Kellermanns, F. W. (2010). The effects of family firm specific sources of TMT diversity: The moderating role of information exchange frequency. *Journal of Management Studies, 47*(2), 322–344.

Ling, Y., Simsek, Z., Lubatkin, M. H., & Veiga, J. F. (2008). Transformational leadership's role in promoting corporate entrepreneurship: Examining the CEO–TMT interface. *Academy of Management Journal, 51*(3), 557–576.

Love, L. G., Priem, R. L., & Lumpkin, G. T. (2002). Explicitly articulated strategy and firm performance under alternative levels of centralization. *Journal of Management, 28*(5), 611–627.

Lubatkin, M. H., Simsek, Z., Yan, L., & Veiga, J. F. (2006). Ambidexterity and performance in small- to medium-sized firms: The pivotal role of top management team behavioral integration. *Journal of Management, 32*(5), 646–672.

Maitlis, S. (2005). The social processes of organizational sensemaking. *Academy of Management Journal, 48*(1), 21–49.

Mantere, S. (2008). Role expectations and middle manager strategic agency. *Journal of Management Studies, 45*(2), 294–316.

March, J. G., & Simon, H. A. (1958). *Organizations.* New York, NY: Wiley.

Marks, M. A., Mathieu, J. E., & Zaccaro, S. J. (2001). A temporal based framework and taxonomy of team processes. *Academy of Management Review, 26*(3), 356–376.

Martin, J. A., & Eisenhardt, K. M. (2010). Rewiring: Cross-business-unit collaborations and performance in multi-business organizations. *Academy of Management Journal, 53*(2), 265–301.

Martin, M. M., & Anderson, C. M. (1998). The cognitive flexibility scale: Three validity studies. *Communication Reports, 11*(1), 1–9.

Mayer, R. C., Davis, J. H., & Schoorman, F. D. (1995). An integrative model of organizational trust. *Academy of Management Review, 20*(3), 709–734.

Mayer, R. C., & Gavin, M. B. (2005). Trust in management and performance: Who minds the shop while the employees watch the boss? *Academy of Management Journal, 48*(5), 874–888.

McGrath, J. E. (1984). *Groups: Interaction and performance.* Englewood Cliffs, NJ: Prentice Hall.

Mintzberg, H. (1973). *The nature of managerial work*. New York, NY: Harper & Row.

Mintzberg, H. (1983). *Structure in fives*. Englewood Cliffs, NJ: Prentice Hall.

Mintzberg, H., Raisinghani, D., & Theoret, A. (1976). The structure of "unstructured" decision processes. *Administrative Science Quarterly 21*(2), 246–275.

Mom, T. J. M., Van Den Bosch, F. A. J., & Volberda, H. W. (2007). Investigating managers' exploration and exploitation activities: The influence of top-down, bottom-up, and horizontal knowledge inflows. *Journal of Management Studies, 44*(6), 910–931.

Nielsen, S. (2010). Top management team diversity: A review of theories and methodologies. *International Journal of Management Reviews, 12*(3), 301–316.

Noble, C. H. (1999). The eclectic roots of strategy implementation research. *Journal of Business Research, 45*(2), 119–134.

Nutt, P. C. (1986). Tactics of implementation. *Academy of Management Journal, 29*(2), 230–261.

Nutt, P. C. (1999). Surprising but true: Half the decisions in organizations fail. *Academy of Management Executive, 13*(4), 75–90.

O'Toole, J., Galbraith, J., & Lawler, E. E., III (2002). When two (or more) heads are better than one: The promises and pitfalls of shared leadership. *California Management Review, 44*(4), 65–83.

Olson, B. J., Parayitam, S., & Bao, Y. (2007). Strategic decision making: The effects of cognitive diversity, conflict, and trust on decision outcomes. *Journal of Management, 33*(2), 196–222.

Peterson, R. S., Smith, D. B., Martorana, P. V., & Owens, P. D. (2003). The impact of chief executive officer personality on top management team dynamics: One mechanism by which leadership affects organizational performance. *Journal of Applied Psychology, 88*(5), 795–808.

Pettigrew, A. M. (1992). On studying managerial elites. *Strategic Management Journal, 13*(8), 163–182.

Priem, R. L., Lyon, D. W., & Dess, G. G. (1999). Inherent limitations of demographic proxies in top management team heterogeneity research. *Journal of Management, 25*(6), 935–953.

Raes, A. M. L., Glunk, U., Heijltjes, M. G., & Roe, R. A. (2007). Top management team and middle managers: Making sense of leadership. *Small Group Research, 38*(3), 360–386.

Raes, A. M. L., Heijltjes, M. G., Glunk, U., & Roe, R. A. (2011). The interface of the top management team and middle managers: A process model. *Academy of Management Review, 36*(1), 102–126.

Rau, D. (2005). The influence of relationship conflict and trust on the transactive memory performance relation in top management teams. *Small Group Research, 36*(6), 746–771.

Rico, R., Sanchez-Manzanares, M., Gil, F., & Gibson, C. (2008). Team implicit coordination processes: A team knowledge-based approach. *Academy of Management Review, 33*(1), 163–184.

Roberto, M. A. (2003). The stable core and dynamic periphery in top management teams. *Management Decision, 41*(2), 120–131.

Rousseau, D. M., Sitkin, S. B., Burt, R. S., & Camerer, C. (1998). Not so different after all: A cross-discipline view of trust. *Academy of Management Review, 23*(3), 393–404.

Russell, C. J. (2001). A longitudinal study of top-level executive performance. *Journal of Applied Psychology, 86*(4), 560–573.

Schilit, W. K., & Paine, F. T. (1987). An examination of the underlying dynamics of strategic decisions subject to upward influence activity. *Journal of Management Studies, 24*(2), 161–187.

Schneider, M. (2002). A stakeholder model of organizational leadership. *Organization Science, 13*(2), 209–220.

Schoorman, F. D., Mayer, R. C., & Davis, J. H. (2007). An integrative model of organizational trust: Past, present, and future. *Academy of Management Review, 32*(2), 344–354.

Senge, P. M. (1990). *The fifth discipline: The art and practice of the learning organization.* New York, NY: Currency Doubleday.

Simons, T. (2002a). Behavioral integrity: The perceived alignment between managers' words and deeds as a research focus. *Organization Science, 13*(1), 18–35.

Simons, T. (2002b). The high cost of lost trust. *Harvard Business Review, 80*(9), 18–19.

Simons, T., Pelled, L. H., & Smith, K. A. (1999). Making use of difference: Diversity, debate, and decision comprehensiveness in top management teams. *Academy of Management Journal, 42*(6), 662–673.

Simons, T., & Peterson, R. S. (2000). Task conflict and relationship conflict in top management teams: The pivotal role of intragroup trust. *Journal of Applied Psychology, 85*(1), 102–111.

Sims, D. (2003). Between the millstones: A narrative account of the vulnerability of middle managers' storying. *Human Relations, 56*(10), 1195–1211.

Smith, K. G., Smith, K. A., Olian, J. D., Sims, H. P. J., O'Bannon, D. P., & Scully, J. A. (1994). Top management team demography and process: The role of social integration and communication. *Administrative Science Quarterly, 39*(3), 412–438.

Spiro, R. J., Feltovich, P. J., Jacobson, M. J., & Coulson, R. L. (1992). Cognitive flexibility, constructivism, and hypertext: Random access instruction for advanced knowledge acquisition in ill-structured domains. In T. M. Duffy

& D. H. Jonassen (Eds.), *Constructivism and the technology of instruction: A conversation* (pp. 57–76). Hillsdale, NJ: Lawrence Erlbaum Associates.

Srivastava, A., Bartol, K. M., & Locke, E. A. (2006). Empowering leadership in management teams: Effects on knowledge sharing, efficacy, and performance. *Academy of Management Journal, 49*(6), 1239–1251.

Steiner, I. D. (1972). *Group process and productivity.* New York, NY: Academic Press.

Tajfel, H., & Turner, J. (1986). The social identity theory of intergroup behavior. In S. Worchel & W. C. Austin (Eds.), *The social psychology of intergroup relations* (pp. 7–24). Chicago, IL: Nelson-Hall.

Talaulicar, T., Grundei, J., & Werder, A. V. (2005). Strategic decision making in start-ups: The effect of top management team organization and processes on speed and comprehensiveness. *Journal of Business Venturing, 20*(4), 519–541.

Tengblad, S. (2002). Time and space in managerial work. *Scandinavian Journal of Management, 18*(4), 543–565.

Tengblad, S. (2006). Is there a "new managerial work"? A comparison with Henry Mintzberg's classic study 30 years later. *Journal of Management Studies, 43*(7), 1437–1461.

Thomas, T., Schermerhorn, J. R., Jr., & Dienhart, J. W. (2004). Strategic leadership of ethical behavior in business. *Academy of Management Executive, 18*(2), 56–66.

Treviño, L. K., Hartman, L. P., & Brown, M. (2000). Moral person and moral manager: How executives develop a reputation for ethical leadership. *California Management Review, 42*(4), 128–142.

Tsui, A. S., Ashford, S. J., Clair, L. S., & Xin, K. R. (1995). Dealing with discrepant expectations: Response strategies and managerial effectiveness. *Academy of Management Journal, 38*(6), 1515–1543.

Tuckman, B. W. (1965). Developmental sequence in small groups. *Psychological Bulletin, 63*, 384–399.

Tushman, M. L., & Nadler, D. A. (1978). Information processing as an integrating concept in organizational design. *Academy of Management Review, 3*(3), 613–624.

Ury, W., & Patton, B. (1991). *Getting to yes: Negotiating agreement without giving in* (2nd ed.). New York, NY: Penguin Books.

Vera, D., & Crossan, M. (2004). Strategic leadership and organizational learning. *Academy of Management Review, 29*(2), 222–240.

Vroom, V. H., & Yetton, P. W. (1973). *Leadership and decision making.* Pittsburgh, PA: University of Pittsburgh Press.

Wageman, R., Nunes, D. A., Burruss, J. A., & Hackman, J. R. (2008). *Senior leadership teams: What it takes to make them great.* Boston, MA: Harvard Business School Press.

Waller, M. J., Gupta, N., & Giambatista, R. C. (2004). Effects of adaptive behaviors and shared mental models on control crew performance. *Management Science, 50*(11), 1534–1544.

Walton, R., & McKersie, R. (1965). *A behavioral theory of labor negotiations.* New York, NY: McGraw-Hill.

Weick, K. E. (1979). *The social psychology of organizing.* New York, NY: McGraw-Hill.

Weick, K. E. (1995). *Sensemaking in organizations.* Thousand Oaks, CA: Sage Publications, Inc.

Weick, K. E., Sutcliffe, K. M., & Obstfeld, D. (2005). Organizing and the process of sensemaking. *Organization Science, 16*(4), 409–421.

Wooldridge, B., & Floyd, S. W. (1990). The strategy process, middle management involvement, and organizational performance. *Strategic Management Journal, 11*(3), 231–241.

Wooldridge, B., Schmid, T., & Floyd, S. (2008). The middle manager perspective on strategy process: Contributions, synthesis, and future research. *Journal of Management, 34*(6), 1190–1221.

Yin, R. K. (2003). *Case study research: Design and methods* (Vol. 5). Thousand Oaks, CA: Sage Publications, Inc.

Index

Announcing the Business Expert Press Digital Library

Concise E-books Business Students
Need for Classroom and Research

This book can also be purchased in an e-book collection by your library as

- a one-time purchase,
- that is owned forever,
- allows for simultaneous readers,
- has no restrictions on printing,
- can be downloaded as PDFs from within the library community.

Our digital library collections are a great solution to beat the rising cost of textbooks. E-books can be loaded into their course management systems or onto students' e-book readers.

The **Business Expert Press** digital libraries are very affordable, with no obligation to buy in future years.

For more information, please visit **www.businessexpertpress.com/librarians**. To set up a trial in the United States, please contact **Sheri Allen** at *sheri.allen@globalepress.com*; for all other regions, contact **Nicole Lee** at *nicole.lee@igroupnet.com*.

OTHER TITLES IN OUR STRATEGIC MANAGEMENT COLLECTION

Series Editor: Mason Carpenter

An Executive's Primer on the Strategy of Social Networks by Mason Carpenter

Building Strategy and Performance Through Time: The Critical Path by Kim Warren

Knowledge Management: Begging for a Bigger Role 2e by Arnold Kransdorff

Sustainable Business: An Executive's Primer by Nancy Landrum and Sally Edwards

Mergers and Acquisitions: Turmoil in Top Management Teams by Jeffrey Krug

Positive Management: Increasing Employee Productivity by Jack Walters

The General Management Process by Jeffrey Krug and Wally Stettinius

Fundamentals of Global Strategy: A Business Model Approach by Cornelis de Kluyver

A Leader's Guide to Virtual Business by John Girard and JoAnn Girard

Building Organizational Capacity for Change: The Leader's New Mandate by William Q. Judge

Dynamic Strategies for Small Businesses by Sviatoslav Steve Seteroff and Lydia Guadalupe Campuzano